Robin Hooper

Robin Hooper is a writer and actor. In the 1980s and 1990s he was Literary Manager for both Paines Plough and the Royal Court Theatre which were instrumental in launching the careers of some of Britain's foremost playwrights and directors.

His previous plays include *The Move* (one of the first NT Platforms to tour), *Astonish Me* (RSC/Almeida Theatre, then Home Theatre off-Broadway), *Queer Fish* (BAC), *Free From Sorrow* (Tristan Bates), *Not the Love I Cry For* (Arcola Theatre), *Love Your Soldiers* (Commission for Sheffield Crucible Studio), and *Foul Pages* (Hope Theatre). As an actor, his television and film credits include the role of Malcolm in *The Office, The Terence Davis Trilogy, Prick up Your Ears, The Children Act, Riot at the Rite, Lucan, Mrs Biggs*, and *Quacks*.

Theatre includes seasons at the Liverpool Everyman and Glasgow Citizen's Theatre, *The Cherry Orchard* (Arcola Theatre), and *Dear Brutus* (Southwark Playhouse).

First published in the UK in 2021 by Aurora Metro Publications Ltd.

67 Grove Avenue, Twickenham, TW1 4HX

www.aurorametro.com   info@aurorametro.com

@aurorametro

Broken Lad copyright © 2021 Robin Hooper.

Cover image courtesy of Alex Brenner and Mihaela Bodlovic © 2021

Production: Cheryl Robson

With many thanks to: Saranki Sriranganathan

Printed in the UK by 4edge Limited on sustainably resourced paper.

ISBNs:

978-1-912430-66-6 (print)

978-1-912430-67-3 (ebook)

BROKEN LAD

by
Robin Hooper

AURORA METRO BOOKS

arcola
theatre

Arcola is one of London's leading off-West End theatres. Locally engaged and internationally minded, Arcola stages a diverse programme of plays, operas and musicals. World-class productions from major artists appear alongside cutting-edge work from the most exciting emerging companies.

Arcola delivers one of London's most extensive community engagement programmes, creating over 5000 opportunities every year. By providing research and development space to diverse artists, Arcola champions theatre that's more engaging and representative. Its pioneering environmental initiatives are internationally renowned, and aim to make Arcola the world's first carbon-neutral theatre.

with thanks to all of our Supporters and Volunteers

Supported using public funding by
ARTS COUNCIL ENGLAND

CAST AND CREATIVES

Liz - Carolyn Backhouse

Phil - Patrick Brennan

Ned - Adrian McLoughlin

Ria - Yasmin Paige

Josh - Dave Perry

Director - Richard Speir

Set and Costume Designer - Cecilia Trono

Lighting Designer - Matthew Swithinbank

Sound Designer - Jamie Lu

Assistant Director - Jessy Roberts

Production Manager - Cat Ryall

Stage Manager - Millie Cousins

Casting Consultant - Ellie Collyer-Bristow CDG

Design Assistant - Sarah Duguid

PR - Kevin Wilson PR

Production Photographer - David Monteith-Hodge

Production Videographer - Savage Mills

BIOGRAPHIES

Carolyn Backhouse - Liz

Liz's theatre credits include *Storm in a Flower Vase* (Arts Theatre); *A Busy Day, Hobson's Choice* (Lyric Theatre); *The Magistrate* (Savoy Theatre); *A Dream of People, The Beaux' Strategem, A Midsummer Night's Dream* (RSC); *Larkin With Women, Leaving* (Havel); *Private View, Greenwash, How To Be Happy, The Actor's Nightmare* (Orange Tree Theatre); *A Midsummer Night's Dream* (Regent's Park Open Air Theatre); *A Pupil, Some Girl(s)* (Park Theatre); *The Notebook of Trigorin* (Finborough Theatre); *Hobson's Choice, Hay Fever, Miranda, Beethoven's Tenth, A Midsummer Night's Dream, The Human Error, Educating Rita, Oleanna* (Chichester Festival Theatre); *A Kind of Alaska* (Bristol Old Vic); *Private Lives, Closer, Racing Demon, Absence of War, Murmuring Judges* (Birmingham Rep); *Hobson's Choice, Larkin With Women* (Stephen Joseph Theatre); *The Merchant of Venice, The Crucible, Time and the Conways, Colombe, French Without Tears, Fallen Angels, Pride and Prejudice* (Salisbury Playhouse); *An Ideal Husband, Pleasure and Repentance* (Theatre Clwyd); *Wait Until Dark* (Plymouth); *Crash* (West Yorkshire Playhouse); *Venus and Adonis* (Orchard Theatre Company); and *Romeo and Juliet* (Hull Truck). National tours include *Octopus Soup, The Handyman, The Governess, Mrs Warren's Profession, Rebecca, Richard ll, Richard lll, The Breadwinner, National Hero, Naked Justice, The Real Thing, Entertaining Angels*, and *Hobson's Choice*. Television includes *Man Down, Rosemary and Thyme, Blue Murder, Midsommer Murders, Hollyoaks, Casualty, The Bill, Heroes and Villains: Full Throttle, Jupiter Moon* (series), *Rides, Absent Friends, Doctors, Coronation*

Street, and *Virgin and Martyr* (TVE). Films include *Brides in the Bath, Robin Hood, A Short Film About John Bolton, Scoop* (Woody Allen), and *Us and Them*. Carolyn has worked extensively on the radio.

Patrick Brennan - Phil

Patrick's theatre credits include *Oedipus, The Reporter, Entertaining Strangers, King Lear, Antony and Cleopatra, Light Shining In Buckinghamshire* (National Theatre); *Macbeth, Twelfth Night, Richard II, Edward II, Measure for Measure, In Extremis, Henry IV Part I & II, Bedlam* (Shakespeare's Globe); *As You Like It, Measure for Measure, Hamlet, Romeo and Juliet, A Clockwork Orange* (Royal Shakespeare Company); *Guys and Dolls* (Donmar); *Othello, Paint Your Wagon, The Big I Am, Fiddler on the Roof, The Conquest of the South Pole, The Sum, Romeo & Juliet* (Liverpool Everyman & Playhouse); *Duchess Of Malfi* (Nottingham Playhouse); *Crouch Touch Pause Engage* (National Theatre of Wales/ Out of Joint); *The Promise* (Orange Tree); *Land Of My Fathers* (Theatre 503); *A Shadow Of A Gunman* (The Kilburn Tricycle); and *Accolade* (Finborough). Television and film credits include *Our House, My Policeman, Carnival Row, Absentia, Shakespeare and Hathaway, Bruno, Downton Abbey, Call the Midwife, Father Brown, Cadfael, Without Motive, Holby City, The Bill, Casualty, Doctors, Caerdydd, Gangsta Granny, Into the Storm, The Children Act, The Globe Live: Richard II, Measure For Measure, Henry IV Part I*, and *Henry IV Part II*. Patrick is a regular contributor to BBC Radio Drama.

Adrian McLoughlin - Ned

Adrian's previous work at Arcola includes *The Rivals* (2014). Theatre credits include *People* (National Theatre tour); *Taking Steps* (Orange Tree Theatre); *Haunting Julia, Life & Beth, A Trip To Scarborough, Drowning On*

Dry Land, Private Fears In Public Places, Joking Apart (Stephen Joseph Theatre); *House & Garden, Singin' In The Rain* (National Theatre); *Lettuce & Lovage, The Crucible* (West Yorkshire Playhouse); *The Odd Couple* (York Theatre Royal); *Things We Do For Love* (Duchess Theatre and tour); *True West* (Salisbury Playhouse); and *Taking Steps* (Derby Playhouse). Television credits include *Holby City* (BBC); *Sandylands* (UKTV); *After Life* (Derek Prods/Netflix); *Black Earth Rising* (Forgiving Earth Ltd); *The Hour* (Kudos); *New Tricks* (Wall to Wall); *Come Fly With Me, Jam and Jerusalem, Pulling Home Again, 15 Stories High, Judge John Deed, Last of the Summer Wine* (BBC); *Kingdom* (Parallel Films); *Longford* (Granada); and *Touch of Frost* (Yorkshire). Films credits include *Alice Through the Looking Glass* (12th Battalion Productions), *The Death of Stalin* (Free Range Films), and *Thunderpants* (Dragon Pictures).

Yasmin Paige - Ria

Theatre credits include *Once Upon a Time in Nazi Occupied Tunisia* (Almeida Theatre); *Leopoldstadt* (Wyndham's Theatre); *Actually* (Trafalgar Studios); *Circle, Mirror, Transformation* (HOME, Manchester); *Ah, Wilderness!* (Young Vic); *Spur Of The Moment* (Royal Court); *Annie* (Hammersmith Apollo); *Romeo & Juliet* (Bloomsbury Theatre); and *Les Misérables* (Palace Theatre). Film credits include *The Souvenir Part II*; *Chicken*; *The Possibilities Are Endless*; *The Double*; *Submarine*; *Ballet Shoes*; *Second Nature*; *Z*; *The Others*; *Wondrous Oblivion*; *Tooth*; *The Keeper*; *I Could Never Be Your Woman*; and *Girl's Club (Aka True True Lie)*. Television credits include *Good Karma Hospital*; *Glue*; *Pramface*; *Coming Up: Spoof or Die*; *The Search*; *Sarah Jane Adventures: The Invasion of the Bane*; *Secret Life*; *Smack The Pony*; *Bed & Breakfast Star*; *Keen Eddie*;

Doctors; *The Last Detective*; *Mysti*; *Golden Hour*; *My Life As A Popat*; and *Murderland*. Radio credits include *Dead in the Water* (BBC Radio 4); *The Meeting Point* (BBC Belfast); *Topic Chocolate Bars* (BBC Radio/ Film 400); and *The Little Toe Radio* (BBC 7).

Dave Perry - Josh

Soon after graduating from LAMDA in 2012, Dave appeared in *Longing* (Hampstead Theatre) alongside Tamsin Greig and Iain Glen, before being invited back to the drama school to perform with graduating students as a professional practitioner. Following this, Dave lead casts in a series of short films for various directors and writers, including *Lifeclass* (Channel 4's Random Acts). Theatre credits include *Sket* (Park Theatre), and *A Chorus of Disapproval, A Servant to Two Masters* (Minack Theatre). Film credits include *A United Kingdom*. An accomplished ballroom dancer, Dave has danced in television series *Vanity Fair* and *Downton Abbey*.

Richard Speir - Director

Richard's theatre credits as a Director include *Gentlemen* (Arcola Theatre); *Byron: Angel & Outcast* (Cadogan Hall and Kazakhstan tour); *Claw Hammer* (SparkHaus); *Spun* (Arcola Theatre); *Moments* (Hen and Chickens); *Stevie* (SLAM); *DEADLOCK, The Nine O'Clock Service* (Theatre503); *Play 2, Breakneck* (Old Red Lion); and *The Inevitable Disappearance of Edward J. Neverwhere* (STAR). As Associate Director, theatre credits include *Witness For The Prosecution* (London County Hall). As Assistant Director, theatre credits include *Kenny Morgan, New Nigerians* and *Gariné* (Arcola Theatre).

Cecilia Trono - Set and Costume Designer

Cecilia's theatre credits include *Gentlemen* (Arcola Theatre); *The Diary of a Scoundrel* (Rose Bruford College);

The Rubenstein Kiss (Southwark Playhouse); *The Curious Case of Benjamin Button* (Southwark Playhouse); *Mites* (Tristan Bates Theatre); and *The Ice Cream Boys, The Last Ones* (Jermyn Street Theatre - Off West End Award for Best Set Design).

Matthew Swithinbank - Lighting Designer

Matthew is a London-based lighting designer and technician from Luxembourg. Having graduated with a Ba(Hons) in Technical Theatre from Mountview Academy of Theatre Arts in 2013, he now works extensively as a technician and lighting designer throughout London, as well as the occasional foray out of the country. Theatre credits include *Kings* (New Diorama); *Fugee & Wasted* (Southwark Playhouse); *A First World Problem and Clickbait* (Theatre503); *Callisto: A Queer Epic* (Arcola Theatre); *Warehouse of Dreams & Beetles From The West* (Lion and Unicorn); *Brass, Around The World In 80 Days, Can-Can!* (Union Theatre); *Safe Sex/On Tidy Endings, Game Theory* (Tristan Bates); *Don't Sleep There Are Snakes* (Park Theatre); *There Is A War, The Secret Marriage* (Jackson's Lane); *Victor Frankenstein* (King's Arms, Salford); *White Rose, Very Pleasant Sensations* (Cockpit); *Jane Eyre, Picnic At Hanging Rock* (Abbaye Neumunster, Luxembourg); and *The Devil His Due* (FEATS2011, Geneva). Matthew spent a large part of the past year as one of a team of technicians building the Arcola Theatre's outdoor venue. www.luxlx.co.uk

Jamie Lu - Sound Designer

Jamie trained at RCSSD MFA Scenography. Sound design credits include: *Tokyo Rose* (Southwark Playhouse/UK Tour); *A Report to an Academy, Butterfly, The Most Beautiful Woman in the World* (Barons Court Theatre); and *Apollonia, Flowers for Algernon, Black Mary Poppins* (Focustage, Chinese Tour).

Jessy Roberts - Assistant Director

Jessy is a director and theatre-maker. Theatre credits as Director include *Girls With Wings & Trauma* (Bomb Factory Theatre); *Hitchhiker* (Rondo Theatre); *I Hate Alone* (The Wardrobe Theatre); *Details of a Hurricane* (BOVTS Online); *When They Go Low* (the egg Theatre Royal Bath); *Messy Eaters* (York Theatre Royal); *Out of Love* (John Cooper Studio Theatre); *Wild Thyme and Heather* (York Theatre Royal); and *Image of an Unknown Young Woman* (The Drama Barn). As Assistant Director, theatre credits include *Horseshoes for Hand Grenades* (East Riding Theatre); *Crimes Camera Action* (Theatre Royal Bath); and *Absolute Scenes* (Bristol Old Vic Theatre School). Jessy is an Associate Writer at Middle Child Theatre, Associate Director at The Rondo Theatre, and Artistic Director of Teastain Theatre.

Millie Cousins - Stage Manager

Millie trained at The Royal Central School of Speech and Drama. Her theatre credits include *Jack and the Beanstalk* (Harlow Playhouse); *Stiletto Beach* (Queen's Theatre Hornchurch); *Starved* (The Hope Theatre); *Exceptional Promise* (The Bush Theatre); *Misterman* (New Wimbledon Studio); *Market Boy* (Union Theatre); *Musical Theatre Showcase* (Fortune Theatre); *Peter Pan* (Princes Theatre); *Apocalypse Laow* (Katzspace); *Millennials: Offended* (Pleasance Theatre); *Little by Little* (Etcetera Theatre); *The Wild Duck* (Almeida Theatre); *In The Heights* (Stockwell Playhouse); and *Down and Out LIVE* (Stone Nest). Millie has also worked as Stage Manager for the Liberation International Music Festival.

ABOUT THE PLAY

'Why did you feel the need to write this?' is a question often asked of the playwright. With *Broken Lad* the launching pad was very practical. I wanted to write a play that might be comparatively easy to produce. I'd just completed an ambitious commission which made enormous demands upon everybody.

So now I would go for a one-room setting, five characters, and almost continuous action. I then finally embraced the challenge of making a piece that wasn't my regular territory, a dysfunctional family, within a work play situation. Richard Speir, whom I'd approached very early on to direct it, very generously gave a reading of it in his family home. Facing the feedback there, it was given a very mixed reception from the wonderful actors gathered.

Not too crestfallen, what kept me going during the redrafting, was not only my confidence with the structure, but Richard's commitment and rigour with the text. I find it difficult, and if I'm honest, unnecessary, to reveal too much what the play is about. That is for the audience to decide, but I have a tendency to be too oblique sometimes, and not 'joining up the dots'. Then Richard announced, in the spring of this year, the Arcola Theatre, where both of us have a long and fruitful association, wanted to stage it in their outside space. He stated categorically it was the perfect venue for it. He's been spot on with everything else, including finding a terrific cast and creative team.

– Robin Hooper

Dedicated to
Ashley Paul Claudius

BROKEN LAD

Robin Hooper

This production was first performed on Wednesday 13th October 2021 at Arcola Theatre, London.

CHARACTERS

PHIL, mid-fifties, a stand-up comedian.

NED, sixties, his friend.

JOSH, early twenties, Phil's lad, an estate agent.

RIA, thirty, Josh's girlfriend, a banker.

LIZ, fifties, Phil's ex-wife, a businesswoman.

Action takes place in a room above 'The Albion Pub'.

Time is the present.

With thanks to April De Angelis, Gary Bleasdale, Steve Brody, Dr Joy Conlon, Geraldine Alexander, Charlotte Brimble, Jim Hooper, Mark Jax, and Dave Perry.

This text went to press before the end of rehearsals and so may differ slightly from the play as performed.

All characters appearing in this work are fictitious.

SCENE 1

Summer Evening.

PHIL looks through a window. Sunlight beams into an upper room of a pub. He closes shabby curtains. He turns away, sits, and pulls out his iphone. Light leaps up to his face. He reads a text and closes it. He looks into a broken mirror above a make-shift dressing table. On it his bulky holdall and full plastic carrier bag.

He stands and flicks on a light. There's an old sofa and on top of it, NED's bag with his tablet inside.

A knock on the door.

PHIL   Ned?

NED enters with an opened bottle of beer and a glass of wine.

PHIL   This place is a shithole.

NED   Twenty booked.

PHIL   They take bookings?

NED   Popular venue.

PHIL   Popular my arse. It's not even on the comedy circuit. It's an old pub once famous for strippers. (*NED hands him the bottle.*) Cheers.

NED   Bottoms up. (*sips his wine.*) Disgusting.

PHIL   Take it back then.

NED   I will on the way down.

PHIL   Twenty eh?

NED   There'll be more on the door. It's Friday night.

PHIL   This is how I started. Queen's Arms. Preston. You don't expect to finish up like this.

NED   Times have changed.

PHIL   Tell me about it. That dickhead Eamon has now got a book out. Sales estimated at nearly half a million. And I'm better than him.

NED   I know.

PHIL   Lucky bastard.

NED   Thought he was a friend?

PHIL   He's abandoned me.

NED   His loss.

PHIL   I sure need you at times like this. *(drinks)* Not the thirteenth today, is it?

NED   No. I've checked. Landlord wants a word by the way.

PHIL   Don't let that prick anywhere near me.

NED   He's very well meaning.

PHIL   Looks like Boris Johnson.

NED   I fancy Boris Johnson.

PHIL   One of many that has finished this country.

NED   I'll make no secret of the fact.

PHIL checks himself out in the mirror.

NED   Big cock apparently.

PHIL   So have I.

NED   Scrotum like a rucksack.

PHIL   Get out.

Knock on the door.

PHIL (*whispers*) I'm not here.

NED   Who is it?

JOSH calls off.

JOSH   Me dad.

NED   Your lad.

PHIL   Tell him there's no sign of me.

NED   I will not.

JOSH   What do you get when you cross a cow with a duck?

NED   He's come to see you.

PHIL (*calling*) 'Milk and Quackers'. (*To NED*) What's he want?

NED   You, Phil. His daddy. (*Calling*) Enter.

JOSH opens the door.

NED   He's decent.

JOSH enters.

JOSH   Neddie!

NED   Hello, Josh.

JOSH   How do you catch a squirrel, Dad?

PHIL   Climb up a tree, and act like a nut.

They hug.

PHIL/JOSH Don't be childish.

JOSH   There's a queue outside.

PHIL   Sad, lonely blokes smoking.

JOSH	What's brown and sticky, Pop?
PHIL	A stick.
NED	Grow up, the pair of you. I'll leave you to it.
PHIL	You know those Russian dolls, Neddie?
NED	I'm really starting to hate them.

PHIL (*with NED and JOSH*) They're so full of themselves.

A group hug.

NED	Will you have another, Boss?
PHIL	Could I? Sorry mate. No cash on me.
NED	Same again?
PHIL	Cheers.
NED	Josh?
JOSH	I'll have a softie. Please.
NED	Crisps? Nuts?
PHIL	Salt and vinegar?
NED	Back in a jiffy.

NED leaves.

JOSH	He loves you still.
PHIL	Only one that does.
JOSH	Come off it.
PHIL	He wants my cock in his mouth.
JOSH	Where there's love.
PHIL	Well, he'll never have it.
JOSH	You love him.
PHIL	Do I, hell?

JOSH   You told me once you did.

PHIL   I was pissed and homeless. And he still wouldn't offer me his floor for the night. Same with your mother. Madam even refused her sofa on one occasion. Couldn't possibly inconvenience her new boyfriend and create a compromising situation. I recall that was the excuse. *(Beat)* In a text.

JOSH   Forgive and forget.

PHIL   I was on my last legs.

JOSH   I bumped into you, Dad? Remember? Outside the betting office?

PHIL   My last fiver.

JOSH   And did you get it back?

PHIL   Over fifty quid. Bought myself a shirt.

JOSH   And not give back the cash you owed me?

PHIL pulls out his wallet and finds a twenty quid note.

JOSH   Don't want it now. Too late.

PHIL   Have it. Go on.

JOSH   Nah.

PHIL   It's my last one.

JOSH   Buy a round. Put your bloody hand in your pocket for once and buy a drink, instead of sponging off Neddie. (*He suddenly takes it.*)

PHIL   Incidentally, I'm still waiting for my Christmas present.

JOSH   I forgot.

PHIL   Broke my heart that did. Didn't get a Father's Day card either.

JOSH   I was moving flats.

PHIL   No excuse *(drinks)*.

JOSH   I'm in tonight.

PHIL   Why?

JOSH   I want to see you up there again.

PHIL   I'm a bit rusty, kid.

JOSH   I need the old favourites to wash over me.

PHIL   How do you stop a dog humping your leg? *(With JOSH again)* Pick him up and suck him off.

JOSH   Can't wait.

PHIL   No new ones, I'm sad to say.

JOSH   Don't care.

PHIL   You've heard it all before.

JOSH   We're here for you. Ned. Ria.

PHIL   So I'm told.

JOSH   We're back together again, by the way. She thinks you're hysterical.

PHIL   What's her mobile number?

JOSH   Get lost.

PHIL   I liked Ria.

JOSH   Feeling was mutual, apparently.

PHIL   I made her laugh. Women enjoy that. Apart from your mother.

JOSH   You did make her laugh.

PHIL   Once. On our honeymoon. When I took my kit off. She said I looked like something from 'Planet

of the Apes.' It was downhill all the way after that.
Even when you were born. After the divorce I still
missed having a woman in my life. I got so depressed
I thought if I could suck myself off I wouldn't leave
the house. And if I had tits, I needn't get out of bed.
My masculine self is slipping away.

*PHIL opens one of his two bags. He pulls out a dressing
gown.*

JOSH   My God.

PHIL   What?

JOSH   The gown.

PHIL   Seen me through some piss awful evenings.
*(He finds 'Percy the Panda,' his lucky mascot, and
kisses him.)* And Good Evening, Percy.

JOSH *(checks his iphone)* Ria's late.

PHIL   Women.

JOSH   She forgot something.

PHIL   Always did.

JOSH   Did she?

PHIL   Often. You said.

A knock on the door.

PHIL *(whispers)* I'm not here.

JOSH   Hello?

NED can be heard outside.

NED *(off, mumbled)* Ned.

PHIL   Who?

JOSH   Who is it?

NED (*off, louder.*) Me. Open up.

JOSH opens the door. NED enters with two bottles, and a big bag of crisps in his teeth. He drops the crisps on the side in front of Percy.

JOSH   Twenty-five.

PHIL   Ridiculous prices.

NED   No. Twenty-five. In.

PHIL   Word clearly has got around.

JOSH   Ria's bringing some friends.

PHIL   Any 'totty'?

JOSH   We're back together again, Ned.

NED   Hooray. *(hands JOSH his soft drink and a glass from his pocket.)*

JOSH   Cheers.

PHIL   You better get down there before Modo starts mauling her to death.

JOSH   Who?

PHIL   Landlord.

NED   Your girly whirly got a new hair cut?

JOSH   That's the one.

NED   She's in the bar.

JOSH   Right. Good luck, Dad. Thanks for the softie, Ned. See you later.

JOSH quickly leaves.

NED   Smashing lad.

PHIL   Hands off.

NED   I don't fancy anybody under forty-five. Thought I'd made that very clear.

PHIL   How old is Boris then?

NED   Who cares? Still has a full head of hair.

PHIL   It's a wig.

NED   If it is, it's a very good one.

PHIL   Should be scalped. Getting it wrong. Getting away with it.

NED   I love him. The blonde bombshell.

PHIL   Why?

NED   He's a showman. Like you.

PHIL   We have absolutely nothing in common.

NED   Matter of opinion.

NED hands PHIL his beer.

PHIL   Bless you.

PHIL again looks at himself in the mirror.

PHIL   My manager wanted me to shave my head.

NED   What for?

PHIL   It might make a difference, he said.

NED   To what?

PHIL   A dwindling career?

NED   Bloody cheek.

PHIL   'Most stand ups now don't look like you.'
'And what do I look like then'? I asked.
'Some fat-head just sacked from 'Curry's?' he said.
I very nearly clocked him.

NED   Managers? What do they know?

PHIL   I'd find somebody else if they would have me.

NED   Things are on the up, Phil.

PHIL   Are they, indeed?

NED   Well, Josh is back with Ria again.

PHIL pulls off his jacket and T-shirt.

NED   Which can't be all bad.

PHIL   If you say so.

PHIL is now naked to the waist. He finds a muscle somewhere to flex.

PHIL   And how does the body grab you, Neddie?

NED   Gorgeous.

PHIL   Have I kept the weight off?

NED   Definitely.

PHIL   How's the face?

NED   Magnificent.

PHIL crouches.

PHIL   Look. *(rotates his backside.)* Mr Whippy. Having a shit.

NED   Mind like a sewer.

PHIL   Here's to energizing filth. Come on, Ned? Who would fancy me?

NED   You know I do. You're like my dad. And my uncles were all big blokes. Guess it's something to do with that. See that belly button!

PHIL It's just a belly button.

NED I want to lick it.

PHIL admires himself in the mirror.

PHIL Look at me. I know I'm stunning. I don't need a new comic angle. People should just sniff the testosterone.

PHIL starts singing and shaking his hips.

PHIL 'Wild thing. You make my heart sing. You make everything groovy...'

Door opens and RIA is standing there. PHIL covers both nipples with his thumbs.

PHIL Just don't know where my nipples are today. They're all over the place. *(Beat)* Please knock before entering an artiste's dressing room.

RIA This dump?

PHIL I'm about to change.

NED Like a butterfly he'll emerge from his chrysalis.

PHIL Good evening, Ria.

RIA Hi.

PHIL You're back I hear.

NED Can I get you something, petal?

RIA Neddie! You got my message?

NED Course I did.

RIA Thank you for agreeing to do this one, treasure.

NED Nothing would stop me. What do you fancy?

RIA   Prosecco, please.

NED   Phil?

PHIL   Another beer would be smashing. Ta.

NED   Coming up.

NED leaves. PHIL and RIA alone. RIA sits at the dressing table and looks in the mirror.

PHIL   New hair?

RIA   You like?

PHIL   Hate it.

RIA   Why?

PHIL   You look like a boy.

RIA   And you're piling the weight on, I see.

PHIL   I've lost a few pounds actually.

RIA   Who says?

PHIL   Ned, earlier.

RIA   He would; he's besotted.

RIA pulls out an e-cigarette.

PHIL   Put it away.

RIA   I will not.

PHIL   Please.

RIA   They're harmless.

PHIL   They're a fire risk.

RIA   And why didn't you reply to my
text?

PHIL   Give me a chance.

RIA   I wanted to put you in the picture.

PHIL   How thoughtful.

RIA starts 'vaping'.

PHIL   Absolutely detest those things.

RIA   They're life savers.

PHIL   My GP says people are checking in to get off the addiction. Apart from anything else, they're naf.

RIA   I think they're very elegant.

PHIL   With hair like that?

RIA   Will you stop going on about my hair?

PHIL   It was beautiful.

RIA   It was dowdy. And I don't do 'dowd' anymore. I've turned my back on 'dowd'.

PHIL   And me it seems.

RIA   Then what am I doing here?

PHIL   You still want to please me?

RIA   Too right, but it's business before pleasure now.

PHIL   Why?

RIA   We made a mistake. An awful mistake. *(Beat)*

PHIL   Did we?

PHIL stands up and takes his trousers off. He's now in his socks and underpants. He finds and opens another beer.

RIA opens the curtain a little, and looks through the window.

RIA   Hope we can work something out.

PHIL   You and me?

RIA   Me and my boyfriend, stupid.

PHIL   Josh was doing fine without you. So was I.

RIA   I'm glad.

PHIL   Why come back and spoil everything? He's a lot tougher than you think. We were best mates again.

RIA   Not what I've heard.

PHIL   Healthy friction between father and son is essential. I reckon all comics are doing it for their dads. Making each other laugh is a bonding ritual. And I swear my stuff got better when he was born. I had somebody to bounce off.

RIA   You hit him.

PHIL   Once. Wouldn't do as he was told. So I landed him one. Not on his head though. Still screamed the place down but I never did it again. From then on we sat down and made each other laugh. Now if that's not a healthy parenting option, I don't know what is. (*Beat*) You wearing knickers?

RIA   One track mind.

PHIL   I'm straight and a bloke. Without a home. Without a career. Without a girl. Life started to fall back into place when you came on the scene. Couldn't believe my luck. Josh would have known soon enough. And got over it.

RIA   So selfish.

PHIL   You? Me? Or him?

RIA   He treats me with some respect.

PHIL   So do I.

RIA   You suck the blood out of me.

PHIL   A few bob, I admit. But then you have got a
good job.

RIA   No excuse to rip me off.

PHIL   That why you ran away?

RIA   Can we please focus on this evening?

PHIL   Take your top off.

RIA   As a woman...

PHIL   Don't even go there.

RIA   As a woman practically half your age, I felt
used. What kind of man does that to a woman? Keep
coming to her for handouts just because she gets up five
days a week and goes to work. And cheats on his own
son. Is it Northern? That type of behaviour? Typical of
working-class males north of Watford?

PHIL   You encourage me.

RIA   I did not make the first move.

PHIL   Shall I tell you for why?

RIA   You can try.

PHIL   Why you ensnared me?

RIA   I'm all ears.

PHIL   Because Josh is a crashing bore. Like his
control-freak mother.

RIA   And you're not?

PHIL   Look at me.

RIA   I'm in no mood.

PHIL   Look at me. *(RIA looks at him.)* I know, I'm a mess.

RIA   I want you to see your doctor.

PHIL   Don't change the subject.

RIA   Did you book an appointment? Like I told you?

PHIL   Leave it. And Josh? I don't need to be told he's fit. But it's what's up here, isn't it? It's where we go. It's how I say stuff. When I say it. It's knowing when to begin the begin, isn't it? It's like the work. It's all about attitude, timing, originality, and most important of all, intent. Josh has no bloody idea. He can sell a property but not win a woman.

RIA   Well, he has, actually. If only you'd listen.

PHIL puts on his gown.

RIA   At last.

PHIL   I could sense it was taking your breath away. *(RIA starts giggling.)* The body.

RIA   Oh yeh?

PHIL drinks.

PHIL   I was told once I was a gay icon.

RIA   Ned, seeking your approval?

PHIL   The last real man standing.

PHIL moves in closer to RIA.

PHIL   And you are young. Youth is on your side. And you have a beauty which terrifies men. An aura, dare I say it, which reduces us chaps to tears and misery and pain and worship. But it's a look which disappears without warning. And will leave a quaint, faded pudding of a face, above a shapeless, withered sack of a body.

RIA   Don't care. I'll be loaded.

PHIL   One day nature will play a very cruel joke on you. As it has done on me. And no amount of cash will change that.

RIA   I'll have work done.

PHIL   And if you carry on drinking the way you do, you won't even get that far.

RIA   Maybe I wouldn't want to. And you're the one knocking it back. Not me.

Knock on the door. RIA looks at her iphone.

PHIL (*whispers*) I'm not here. (*Beat*) Tell them then.

RIA   Do your own dirty work.

Knock even louder.

PHIL   This is my sanctuary. This hovel is all I've got for the moment. (*Calling*) Go away. (*Whisper*) Might be Josh, I suppose.

RIA   It won't be.

PHIL   You can see through doors then?

RIA   My friends are keeping him busy.

PHIL   Why?

RIA   So I could talk to you.

PHIL   Cunning, you see.

RIA   They'll text me when he's on the look-out.

Pause.

PHIL   All clear? (*Beat*) He did miss you.

RIA	Did he?
PHIL	Inconsolable. I did too. I've still got nobody.
RIA	You've got Ned.
PHIL	Ned?
RIA	He's your guardian angel.
PHIL	He's a twat.
RIA	More than a lot of men have your age. Nurse-maid? Carer? One decent friend in the world?
PHIL	I've got loads of mates.
RIA	Who?
PHIL	Eamon?
RIA	You won't see much of him anymore.
PHIL	He texts me from time to time.
RIA	He's about to become a big TV star.
PHIL	How do you know?
RIA	Internet. Google him.
PHIL	But he's too...
RIA	What?
PHIL	...Old.
RIA	Younger than you, sweetheart.
PHIL	He's not, actually.
RIA	He looks it.
PHIL	Back off.
RIA	The pilot to his new series is on YouTube.

PHIL   It's not a series, actually. He's fronting a male grooming competition.

RIA   And it's gone viral.

PHIL's head sinks onto the table.

PHIL   I'm... tired. Fucked. Finished.

RIA   You're drinking too much. That's all.

PHIL   I'm about to do a show.

RIA   Then every reason not to.

PHIL   Where's my booze? I'll go down and get it myself. Exercise will do me good.

RIA   No you won't. Your public are down there.

PHIL   Half a dozen.

RIA   Some of them are my mates.

PHIL   Send them home. I'll be a waste of space.

RIA   I've told them all about you.

PHIL   Haven't done a gig for six months. Ready to jump out of that window.

RIA   Phil? Are you really?

PHIL   Of course I am. Tonight's going to be an almighty disaster.

RIA   Now stop it.

PHIL   Josh's in. You.

RIA   Your manager...

PHIL   No he isn't.

RIA   Why not?

PHIL   He dropped me.

RIA   Why?

PHIL   Why does a rat leave a sinking ship? He said he'd taken me as far as he could and felt I needed someone else to push me to the next level. *(Beat)* I did have a one-night stand with his missus. Maybe he was less forgiving than I first thought. *(Beat)* Come on, he'd had enough. The usual. Anyway, he wasn't right for me. Who would be, at my age?

PHIL reaches out to her with his hand.

PHIL   A kiss, Ria? Now? Just the one? Please?

RIA goes to kiss him. But then her iphone pings. A text.

RIA   Josh's on his way.

PHIL   Who cares?

RIA   And they want you to give the room a once over.

PHIL   Who is texting you, may I ask?

RIA   Julia.

PHIL   Who's she?

RIA   My new best friend.

PHIL   Does she wear spectacles?

RIA   She does, actually. For work.

PHIL   Television?

RIA   Where she started. Now owns a big talent management company.

PHIL   Julia Trevis?

RIA   Correct. Rolling in it.

PHIL   You're joking?

RIA   In the bar.

PHIL   No way.

RIA   It took hours to persuade her. She should be at some awards ceremony. I managed to get her here.

PHIL   Why invite her?

RIA   To start planning your comeback.

PHIL   Why?

RIA   Because there's nobody to touch you.

RIA closes her mobile.

PHIL   Bless you.

RIA   For years I've wanted to know and thank you for all the joy you've given to folks like me. You changed my life. Several of my school friends felt the same. All at the shrine of Phil Jessup.

PHIL   Were they wearing white calf-length stockings?

RIA   Yes, but I couldn't afford them.

PHIL   Then let me make it up to you.

RIA   You can't.

She then kisses him playfully on the cheek. NED knocks on the door.

NED (*calling*) It's me.

PHIL and RIA break. NED enters with the drinks. RIA grabs her Prosecco from NED.

RIA   Thanks, babes.

RIA leaves. Silence.

NED puts PHIL's beer down, potters and shakes out a shirt. PHIL sits and checks his iphone.

NED   If you've touched her, you won't see me for dust.

PHIL   Why?

NED   Only a monster would do that to his son.

PHIL   Dry up.

PHIL then stares at himself in the mirror.

SCENE 2

Twenty minutes later. NED, holding the shirt, with LIZ.

They focus on JOSH, finishing his set.

JOSH   'I'm looking for my ex-girlfriend's killer. No one will do it.' And that's my set. First ten minutes or so.

NED   Well done.

JOSH   Thanks Ned.

NED   Is it your own material?

JOSH   You bet.

NED   What got you started?

JOSH   Having a few drinks with the lads then getting up at the office party. Talking about TV shows to potential buyers while driving to viewings. A good ice-breaker that. 'What makes you laugh?' and so on. And watching Dad of course.

NED   But there's nothing of him in it.

JOSH   I go the opposite way to Dad. All the choices he makes, I do the opposite.

LIZ   Bravo.

NED   He can be funny, your old man. But you're right.

JOSH   I value your opinion, mate. Cheers.

NED   You should still show it to Phil.

LIZ   Why?

NED   He understands this business inside out.

LIZ   He'd tear it to shreds.

JOSH   The days when most comedians spent their lives in scaggy pubs, pint in hand, fighting off hecklers and choking on cigarette smoke, are over.

LIZ   With one notable exception.

JOSH   Social media is now helping a new generation of comics. I use Twitter as a baseline filter for jokes. I find out what folks are interested in, and then go from there, inventing on the way. Who knows? One day, bigger try outs on stage. Hopefully the odd TV appearance. Then watch me fly.

NED's iphone pings. He has a text.

NED   Excuse me. Landlord says I can use his iron. Nice to see you Liz.

NED leaves quickly with the shirt, closing the door.

LIZ   Creep. *(Beat)* This room is giving me a migraine.

JOSH   Sorry, Mom.

LIZ   I mean what's it for?

JOSH   Landlord's got plans for it apparently.

LIZ   Smells like a birdcage. I'm off.

JOSH   You've only just got here.

LIZ   I'll spend a penny and disappear into the night.

JOSH   Don't go, Mom.

LIZ   I've no reason to stay, quite frankly.

JOSH   Yes, you have.

LIZ   Why invite me?

JOSH   Wait a minute.

LIZ   Where is he, by the way?

JOSH   Betting Office. Next door.

LIZ   Obviously, why he agreed to this squalor. Can I get you a drink? On my way out?

JOSH   Softie, please. Listen, Mom...

LIZ   You still haven't answered my question. Why ask me here?

JOSH   This evening is important, OK? *(looks at his iphone.)* I think Dad would like to see you.

LIZ   We haven't spoken for months.

JOSH   It's like a graveyard down there.

LIZ   Couldn't give a monkey's.

JOSH   Hardly anybody in.

LIZ   When we first met, he could fill the Palladium. Serves him right.

JOSH   No, it doesn't. He's good. Bloody good.

LIZ   How can I make a difference? Can't be the reason you texted me. Remember I was booked this evening. Tell me. Why were you so keen to see me?

JOSH   Ria and me are back together again. I wanted you, of all people, to join in the fun. To celebrate.

JOSH's iphone pings.

LIZ   Do put that phone away, Josh. Please. And talk to me.

JOSH smartly pockets his iphone. LIZ hugs JOSH.

LIZ   Thank you. I now understand why you've cheered up considerably.

JOSH   Now you tell me.

LIZ   What?

JOSH   Do you think I can do it?

LIZ   What?

JOSH   Stand up?

LIZ   Does it matter what I think?

JOSH   Come on.

LIZ   Of course, you bloody can.

JOSH   Hooray.

LIZ   But what do you propose to do with it?

JOSH   Watch this space.

LIZ   And why give up everything you've fought for, worked for, sacrificed? To go down that route? I always wanted the very best for you.

JOSH   It's in my blood.

LIZ   No denying that, unfortunately.

JOSH   It's the only time I feel alive.

LIZ   And what about Ria?

JOSH   How does *she* feel?

LIZ   Yes. I am interested.

JOSH   She's a fan. Of both Dad and me, obviously. She organised all this. Tonight.

LIZ   So she's responsible?

JOSH   She's got important people in to kick start Dad's career.

LIZ   Who exactly?

JOSH   Julia Trevis.

LIZ   Never heard of her.

JOSH   You will do.

LIZ   But how can she help you?

JOSH   She might. You never know.

LIZ   Phil was always surrounded by dead-beats. And look where it got him.

JOSH   That's all about to change.

LIZ   Is it? Who says?

JOSH   Ria wants Dad to be a success again. And recover. Good on her, I say.

LIZ   And you want her to do the same for you?

JOSH   One day.

LIZ breaks the cuddle.

LIZ   It would finish me if you became something I hoped to see the back of.

JOSH   Oh thanks a bunch.

LIZ   Out of order, I admit.

JOSH   We will make it work.

LIZ   Whatever you choose to do, and it's your life, I recommend a safety net.

JOSH   Always go back to the day job. If I have to.

LIZ   Don't rely on a marriage to support you. Fatal. That's my experience.

JOSH   Heard that one before.

LIZ   I'll stick around then. And do everything I can to help. Diet Coke?

JOSH   Thanks, Mom.

LIZ   Still on the wagon? That's my boy.

LIZ kisses JOSH then leaves, closing the door.

JOSH stands alone, silent, then glances at himself in the mirror. He pulls out an antiseptic hand tissue, wipes his hands and cleans the mirror. He then doesn't know what to do with it, so pockets it. He quietens and again faces the mirror.

JOSH   'Ladies and Gentlemen, put your hands together for Josh Jessup.' Applause. Applause. 'I was thinking. Is it the beard and spectacles? That makes paedophiles so attractive to kids?'

A knock on the door. NED returns with the shirt ironed.

NED   Not back yet?

JOSH   Dad? No.

NED   Great. We can have a catch up.

NED puts PHIL's shirt on a fold up hanger.

JOSH   You still do Dad's shirt?

NED   Quickly run the iron over, yes.

JOSH   That's so kind.

NED   I'm his biggest fan.

JOSH   Apart from Ria, of course. (*Beat*) Got something to show you.

NED   More material?

JOSH   No. Look.

JOSH pulls out an engagement ring.

JOSH   For my girl.

NED   How could you afford that?

JOSH   Bonus pay. I'm going to propose. I feel the moment is right.

NED   You sure, she's the one? She's older than you. She'll boss you about.

JOSH   Might quite like that.

NED   She left me a pushy text insisting I be here. I needed no persuasion. You should focus on your career.

JOSH   First, I need a woman in my life. A way out.

NED   She doesn't play the field, does she?

JOSH   Eh?

NED   Still, who am I to talk?

JOSH   What you heard? Out with it, Neddie.

NED   Nothing. Honest.

NED has pulled out a tablet from his bag. He opens up and clicks onto a site.

JOSH   Then why say such a thing?

NED   In many respects she's a lovely lass. But she's got a roving eye. She's not the same as you. Reliable. Loyal. Caring.

JOSH   If we were too much alike, I wouldn't fancy her. Would I?

NED's screen brightens further. His attention now becomes slightly divided.

JOSH   Thought of her going with another man fills me with terror. Doesn't that prove something?

NED   That's more like an addiction than a romance.

JOSH   The earth moves when we climb into bed together. More than that, the planet goes into orbit. Never felt like that before. *(Beat)* And the simple stuff. Seeing her face on the pillow first thing in the morning. When I get a text from her my heart skips a beat. You must have been there, Neddie?

NED   Can't remember. You give it a few more months, Josh.

JOSH   Too dodgy to wait any longer.

NED   You're still a baby. Have fun. Work at your act. Thought about the Edinburgh Festival? If not this year, next?

Now NED's screen has caught JOSH's attention.

JOSH   Blimey. What a bunch. All these geriatrics up for it?

NED   Love is not old, boy.

JOSH   Are there more sites like this?

NED   Quite a few.

JOSH   What's this?

NED   'Thongs ancient and modern'. Here you have the gay boys who are looking for daddies. Lads broken by lack of love and understanding. I prefer them a lot older myself. Middle aged. Let's go to 'Gerontius'.

JOSH   There are hundreds. They look like Dad. Not got a profile on there, has he?

NED   Hello? 'Mates from the States.'

JOSH   Living here?

NED   Let me check them out. 'We came to Europe looking for foreskins.'

JOSH   Jesus. They're desperate.

NED   They're seeking for life partners before it's too late. Wouldn't you? Adventure before dementia?

PHIL enters. NED closes his tablet.

PHIL   I'm out of here.

NED   I've ironed your shirt. We'll leave now and you can practise. Come on, Josh.

PHIL   That room downstairs? A Victorian monstrosity. I'm reduced to doing gigs in a morgue.

NED   With all that glass and brass it reminds me of the old Empire.

PHIL   What do you know?

JOSH   This is so unprofessional. So much depends...

PHIL   Enough. The pair of you. I know you both mean well. But the omens are bad tonight. Mental.

(Beat) And I've been told a pack of lies as usual. All that's down there are two nuns and a dead wasp.

JOSH   We'll fill it. Somehow.

PHIL takes off the gown. He grabs the ironed shirt and puts it on. Both NED and JOSH pull out their iphones.

JOSH   I'll try a few mates from work.

NED   I'll poach some from the 'Hen and Chickens'.

PHIL   Save your energy. They'll have better things to do.

NED   You'll bring smiles to their faces, as usual.

PHIL   I'm not interested in smiles. I want volume. Volume. And I won't get that this evening. I'm out of here.

Packing up PHIL forgets Percy hidden behind the bag of crisps.

NED   You can't.

PHIL   Can't what?

NED   Walk out.

PHIL   Watch me.

NED   We made a deal with the landlord.

PHIL   Who's we?

NED   Me and Ria.

PHIL   That is illegal. I have a manager. That's his job.

NED   You don't have a manager.

JOSH   No?

NED   Not anymore.

PHIL   Correct. My memory's going. I dumped him.

NED   No Phil. He dumped you.

PHIL   Utter another word, and I'll kick your teeth in. I was told this was a charity gig. To get me on the rails again. This is the first I've heard about deals and God knows what.

NED   You have to do the show.

JOSH   Show must go on, Pop.

PHIL is leaving.

PHIL   Bunch of amateurs. Goodnight.

JOSH stands at the door.

JOSH   No way.

PHIL   Move.

JOSH   You're just looking for an excuse.

PHIL   Excuse?

JOSH   Come on, Dad.

PHIL   Excuse for what?

JOSH   To give up. Do a runner. Because you're bottling it.

PHIL   You can think what you like.

JOSH   You owe it to us. Ria. And Mom.

PHIL   Mom what?

JOSH   Here. Downstairs.

PHIL   Who told Liz? You did, didn't you? What's she after?

JOSH　　　　She was dead keen to see you.

PHIL　　　　Lies. All lies. She's on the prowl. Ready to meddle.

NED　　　　Tonight is for the family as much as anything, Phil.

PHIL　　　　Family? This is nothing to do with family. Why invite that bitch?

JOSH　　　　Can you give us five, Ned?

NED　　　　With pleasure. Get stuck in, Josh.

NED leaves closing the door.

JOSH　　　　Don't call Mom a bitch.

PHIL　　　　Call her what the hell I like.

JOSH　　　　She got me through school.

PHIL　　　　So?

JOSH　　　　She got me through business college.

PHIL　　　　So?

JOSH　　　　She got me my first job.

PHIL　　　　She can pull strings, Liz. I accept that. But our current situation is because of the likes of her.

JOSH　　　　What situation?

PHIL　　　　Decline of the Western world.

JOSH　　　　You can't blame Mom for that.

PHIL　　　　Her sort have a lot to answer for. And do you know what Hitler said?

JOSH　　　　Hitler? Bit of a leap there, Dad.

PHIL   In his bunker, hours before he killed himself? My father warned me. 'It will be the rituals of the East that will destroy us'. *(Beat)* The chickens are coming home to roost, buster, the more we've buried our heads in the sand. And your mother's sort are responsible.

JOSH   Without her, I would be on the streets.

PHIL   And I've been there, pal. Only one of us that has. Last refuge of the working class, ex-soldiers, and true radicals.

JOSH   You did pretty well with Mom until she found out you were a bullshitter.

PHIL   Oh thanks for that.

JOSH   'I'm going to do this. And I'm going to do that.' And look where you are.

PHIL   I've got my pride, Josh. Please don't take that away from me.

JOSH   Then get out there and do what you do best. If not, find something else instead of bemoaning the past. Everybody is bending over backwards to make this work. For months you've been saying, if only somebody would give me another chance. No matter how small. And here it is. The perfect opportunity. And you're too much of a coward to embrace it.

PHIL   I'm no fool, Josh.

JOSH   I'd jump at the opportunity.

PHIL   You?

JOSH   Bored with my job, to be honest. Any excuse. A gig? Here? Even here? Wild horses wouldn't stop me.

PHIL   Well, I just have to be more realistic. My class has taught me...

JOSH   Don't give me that.

PHIL   Unlike your mother, I do not tell myself in a crisis, I have an invisible crown. I wouldn't be seen dead in one. I've slipped up badly agreeing to this.

JOSH   You destroy everything.

PHIL   If you think so.

JOSH   You take the joy out of life. Instead of bringing it in.

PHIL   I'll remember that.

RIA enters abruptly without knocking. Both PHIL and JOSH seem unsettled by this.

PHIL   Knock.

RIA   Sorry.

JOSH   Manners?

PHIL   Please knock before entering, love.

JOSH   He might have been starkers.

PHIL   Ready and waiting.

Pause.

RIA   Excuse me.

PHIL   You're excused.

RIA   Julia is really looking forward.

PHIL   I don't care.

RIA   Ned says you're running away.

PHIL   Once and for all, I am not running away.

RIA   So you are going on?

PHIL   No. And that's the last of it.

JOSH   You're seriously letting the side down, Dad. Please.

PHIL   And I do not want any more emotional blackmail. Apologies Ria. He's been having heart to hearts with his long-suffering mother.

JOSH   You married her so she could do all the problem solving. No wonder she had the common sense to kick you out. And after she did, you fell apart. Yet again, claiming Mom felt she was superior, and it was all a class issue. Well, it isn't. What we have here is a loser. My own father. And it fills me with shame to witness it. Not pity.

PHIL   Not in front of the girlfriend. Please.

Silence except for the street outside.

RIA   He doesn't mean it, Phil.

PHIL   Want a bet?

RIA *(to JOSH)* Go downstairs and calm down.

JOSH   I'm staying here and keeping an eye on you.

RIA pushes cash in JOSH's hand. PHIL clocks this.

RIA   Buy Ned a drink. I'll have a vodka and coke. Be with you in a second.

JOSH   No way. I'm not leaving you alone with him.

RIA   Why not?

JOSH   He'll jump on you.

PHIL looks at RIA.

PHIL   What makes you say that?

RIA *(to JOSH)* Go on. I can look after myself. Go!

JOSH reluctantly leaves. RIA closes the door. PHIL's bags are packed. He wears his jacket over the freshly ironed shirt. PHIL takes his bags in each hand. He hesitates.

RIA   Well, what's stopping you?

PHIL   You.

RIA   No Phil.

PHIL   Come with me.

RIA   Where?

PHIL   We'll find somewhere.

RIA   Your rented bedsit in Mile End?

PHIL   Not possible. Landlord has kicked me out.

RIA   Need I ask why?

PHIL   Couldn't pay my rent. I said I'd get it to him. After tonight. But he wasn't having it. So... I'm homeless. Your place?

RIA   I'm sharing at the moment.

PHIL   Does she wear spectacles and work in a library?

RIA   She does as a matter of fact.

PHIL   Then please take me home, doll, and we'll have a threesome.

RIA   I might, but her girlfriend's an Olympic weight-lifter.

PHIL   Does she wear spectacles?

RIA   She'll eat you for breakfast.

PHIL   All girls together, eh? Never mind. I sense it's a 'no'. Ta-ra then.

RIA   You are not going anywhere, Phil.

PHIL   Just said goodbye to thirty on the races. Haven't got a penny to my name. Help me out. Please.

PHIL drops his bags on the floor. He opens his arms.

PHIL   Prove to me that you love me. Come on.

RIA   You flatter yourself. I've never loved you.

PHIL   You wooed Josh to get to me.

RIA   I had no idea you were his father.

PHIL   Not true.

RIA   We'd been seeing each other for at least a month, before he even mentioned your name. And he was the one who insisted I meet you.

PHIL   Is that what you see in him? Found you a flat, gave you a home, and knocked off his commissioning fee?

RIA   Did I say that?

PHIL   Then gave you one? He's worse than me.

He picks up his bags, goes to the door and opens it. He forgets Percy.

RIA   Please... If you walk out... Julia will never speak to me again.

PHIL   She has absolutely no taste that woman. She'd have no time for an old-fashioned, straight dude like me. Wasting my time as usual.

RIA   You give me no alternative then. If you leave, and not... *(notices the door is wide open.)* You've left the door wide open.

PHIL   I've got nothing to hide.

RIA checks the corridor, then closes the door.

RIA   If you go...

PHIL   Let me think...

RIA   Let me finish.

PHIL   You will rat on me? Go ahead. But do call me if you change your mind and decide to join me on a train to Manchester.

RIA   Back to your roots eh? Sad.

PHIL   Mom and Dad are long gone but there's a good comedy scene there. Always has been. And on second thoughts. Don't waste your breath with lover boy. I'll text him myself from Euston. I'll fill him in about us with pleasure. And the frequent girl on girl episodes in your coke-driven life.

RIA   Try it.

PHIL   Nobody wants to be spoken to like that. Especially their own flesh and blood.

PHIL leaves, still not closing the door. RIA remains.

She checks her iphone then throws it down on the dressing table. She sits in PHIL's chair, then checks herself in the mirror. JOSH enters and smartly closes the door behind him.

JOSH   You two finished?

RIA   What?

JOSH   He gave you a look.

RIA   When? Who?

JOSH   Pop.

RIA picks up her iphone.

RIA   Cheer up.

JOSH   I might.

RIA   Where's my drink?

JOSH   In a minute. *(Beat)* Where's Dad gone?

RIA   Betting shop?

JOSH   Are you happy?

RIA   I am now. Very. You?

JOSH   I was.

RIA   He will go on tonight. So stop fretting.

JOSH   It's not that.

RIA   What is it, then?

JOSH   That look he gave you. When I left earlier? My own father. He's such an old lecher.

RIA   I wouldn't know.

JOSH   Maybe this isn't the time and the place...

RIA   What for?

JOSH   A chat. A proper catch up. Urgent.

RIA   I'm willing. Off you go then.

JOSH   Ned might nip in any minute.

RIA   He's disappeared.

JOSH   Him as well?

RIA   He was on his phone a lot.

JOSH   Drumming up an audience. Him and the landlord are doing well. A few out there who remember him from his TV days. The house might be on the mature side but who cares?

RIA   He's a saint. *(Beat)* So? I'm not sitting here all night when I need to be looking after my friends. Spit it out.

JOSH   Why?

RIA   I'm not a mindreader. Why what?

JOSH   Why did we finish this in the first place?

RIA   Why go back, Josh?

JOSH   The reason?

RIA   Old ground.

JOSH   Is it?

RIA   Right. I needed some air.

JOSH   What kind of air? Bad? Fresh? What? Why?

RIA   Dunno really.

JOSH   Right. You said you felt crowded. How come? I was away for nearly two months to look after gran'. Didn't you get a big bucket full of air then? When Mom found her a decent care home I came straight back. And you were a different woman.

RIA   Had a hair-cut. So?

JOSH   Is that all? That and colouring it, often means a change of heart.

RIA   Who says? Don't tell me. I can guess. Mommy?

JOSH   Was it the parents? Were they spying on you? I didn't ask them to? Was that it? Weird lot my family. (*Beat*) Still I can be obsessive at times. Clingy. Average. I know it.

RIA   No you're not.

JOSH   I never really understood why we split. And one day you said you'd tell me.

RIA   I've told you.

JOSH   The truth?

Pause. RIA uses her e-cigarette and vapes.

RIA   Now, is not the time.

JOSH   I think it is.

RIA   Later maybe.

JOSH   So there is something?

RIA   I need a drink.

JOSH   I need to know. Why Dad looked at you that way?

RIA   How should I know?

JOSH   And you looked at him.

RIA   People do when they're having a conversation.

JOSH   This wasn't a chat, Ria. That moment.

RIA   What was it then?

JOSH   More like a massive recognition.

RIA   Can't imagine what you're getting at here.

JOSH   In the past...

RIA   Something Fat-Face always talks about. Note. A habit you normally hate.

JOSH   Fat-Face? That's very familiar. You calling him Fat-Face?

RIA   Pretty common name for a bloke who's on the big side.

JOSH   But you don't really know Phil that well do you? Do you? Even though you came charging into his dressing room without knocking?

RIA   I've invested a lot in this evening.

JOSH   So it seems. Why?

RIA   So have you.

JOSH   But you were the one who organised the gig in the first place. You're the reason why we're all in this pub tonight. Pretty strange when you look into it.

RIA   He's brilliant at his job. Something I really appreciate. And others. You never shut up about him.

JOSH   Don't I?

RIA   You have occasionally bored me rigid. But we do when we love somebody. Talk about them. Too much. *(She stands.)* Let me go.

JOSH   Let you go?

RIA   Let me sort out my friends. We can deal with this later.

JOSH   There's quite a bit, actually.

RIA   I'm all fucking ears.

JOSH   Don't swear at me.

RIA   Why not?

JOSH   I hate it when a woman swears.

RIA   Then you'd better get used to it. Because at this fucking rate...

JOSH   You had an affair, didn't you?

RIA   Who with?

JOSH   You and Phil.

RIA   Josh?

JOSH   Somebody else? Tell me the truth.

RIA   I always tell you the truth.

JOSH   There was a look.

RIA   You keep on saying.

JOSH   A real connection between you. I've noticed it before. Brushed it aside. But never thought I would see it again. Then I did this evening. There it was. As clear as daylight. I'm no idiot, Ria.

RIA   No idea what you're on about.

JOSH   You swear to me.

RIA   I swear to you.

JOSH   That he's never touched you?

RIA   I swear.

NED enters.

NED *(to RIA)* You're needed downstairs, lovely. There's a mass of people looking for you. Including the hideous Eamon Eliot.

JOSH   What's he doing here?

RIA   Julia invited him. He might open doors.

JOSH *(to RIA)* You've really done your homework, haven't you?

NED Don't tell Phil. If you can find him.

RIA leaves but forgets her e-cigarette.

NED It's filling up at last. Hoorah.

NED opens up his tablet again. JOSH stands by the window. He opens the curtain. As he does so he seems to keel over. NED goes to JOSH.

NED What is it, lad?

JOSH Like everything else. I'll have to get over it.

NED What? I'm listening.

JOSH I want to kill him.

NED Phil?

JOSH I'll kill the bastard.

NED What's he done?

JOSH Ruined my fucking life.

NED Josh?Josh?

JOSH I want to kill myself.

NED Cry it out.

JOSH Finish it.

NED Cry it out.

NED now holds JOSH.

JOSH He stole my girl.

NED No, he hasn't.

JOSH That's why she left me.

NED   But she's back again.

JOSH   Only minutes ago, she wanted me out the room to fuck him.

NED   Here? Nah.

JOSH   I'll push a knife through his heart.

NED   Then what?

JOSH   Don't give a toss.

NED   You'll go to jail.

JOSH   He won't get away with it. Why I had to be here. Had to check it out. My doubts were confirmed when even Ria herself was helping to organise this fiasco. Full on.

NED   We all are. We all care for him really.

JOSH   Why?

NED   We love him. Despite everything, when he goes out there, he gives body and soul. And we just have to accept he's what the best people in this business regard themselves.

JOSH   What?

NED   Numero Uno.

JOSH   Numero what?

NED   Numero Uno.

JOSH   Oh get a life, Ned.

NED   Only trying to help. This bloody family. Christ.

JOSH *(breaks away)* Always on his side because you want it up the arse.

NED   Chance would be a fine thing.

JOSH   Going down there and cut his cock off. Then shove it down his throat.

NED   You'll have us kicked out. And your mom's downstairs.

JOSH   She'll be more than happy to join in.

NED   Then the two of you, why not kill him after the show? Or during it. Finish him with a bit of style. Unless he has a heart attack first.

NED returns to his tablet, flicking on the screen. It lights up.

JOSH   Numero bloody Uno? Is that Italian for dead meat?

NED focuses on his screen.

NED   It really means what he's like inside. Deep deep inside. He puts himself and his own needs first. Not unlike our Boris. Desperate to be loved. And why? Because Phil's a very frightened man.

JOSH   He screwed my girlfriend. I know he has. Why would *he* be frightened of *me*?

NED   Because you've learnt to face him.

JOSH   Only because I've wanted more.

NED   And sadly your dad will never give it you. He knows that. And perhaps it's about time you did. Learn to accept he's never going to put you first. And you'll get by. Like a lot of lads on this planet.

JOSH   Even down to affairs of the heart?

NED   Especially affairs of the heart.

JOSH   Why's that?

NED   Because Phil, sadly, is in love with himself. And he's a show off. He's crafted a personality disorder into a trade. A career. And after all the ups and downs he's been through, he knows the only way he can really survive is to get back in the saddle again, go out there and speak the truth of it. *(Beat)* Genuine love is about... well... God knows.

NED then clicks on a particular site.

A brighter light hits his face.

JOSH   You're over sixty-five, mate.

NED   A pensioner. Don't have to tell me.

JOSH   You should have some idea by now.

NED   I'm a late developer.

JOSH   Still. Wouldn't recommend it: Love.

NED stares at his screen. JOSH checks his iphone.

JOSH   We've seen the last of him.

NED   Think so?

JOSH   No text.

NED   He'll be back. He's forgotten his lucky mascot. Look. Left Percy on the side.

JOSH finds Percy behind the large bag of crisps. He hangs onto him.

NED   Phil is very superstitious. He won't go far without Percy.

JOSH   Does he know?

NED   Oh yes.

JOSH   So he is on his way?

NED   He wanted me to forward him. I refused.

JOSH   Ned, you are a miracle worker.

NED   We'll see.

NED remains preoccupied with his screen. JOSH, still holding Percy, moves to the window to get some air.

JOSH   When I was five, Dad once left me on the pavement. Busy Shopping Centre. A Saturday. Football fans. Drunks. Terrorists. We were out buying me new trainers. Mom's money, as usual, but the present was meant to be from him. And he simply forgot me. Left me there. A traffic warden walked me home. *(Beat)* What if Dad just collects Percy and vanishes.

NED   He won't.

JOSH   How can you be so sure?

NED   His old manager turned up. Had second thoughts.

JOSH   Won't make any difference.

NED   Now do you want your dad to do this gig? Think positive. That's why we're all here. To get him on there again.

JOSH   Then I'll finish him. If all goes to plan.

NED   What plan?

JOSH   I've come prepared. A lesson Mom taught me. You just watch.

JOSH throws Percy back on the dressing table and leaves.

NED looks at his phone. Then at his screen.

NED Hello? 'Dalston Paul?' Well Percy Panda? (*He clicks.*) A flicker of interest. A wink in my mail box? Oh, the mystery. Give him one back? What's there to lose?

He keys in a wink. Then PHIL enters. Silence. PHIL quietly puts Percy into his bag.

PHIL Unforgivable, Ned. That you wouldn't do this last favour for me?

NED Only way I could bring you back.

PHIL I've no intention of sticking around.

NED Oh please yourself then.

PHIL Hope all goes well this evening.

NED It will.

PHIL I really don't think so.

NED I know so.

PHIL Oh don't tell me. They've found a replacement.

NED Landlord got his act together.

PHIL Ugly mug's not going on, is he?

NED Asked around and Josh is.

PHIL Josh?

NED Offered to go on.

PHIL He's not a comic.

NED We'll see.

PHIL He can't do stand-up. He's too good-looking.

NED   Oh yes he can. He's been practising. For years, he tells me. On the quiet.

PHIL   I had no idea.

NED   Understandable, I suppose. Didn't want to steal your thunder.

PHIL   Nobody. But nobody. Not even my own son, could steal that, my friend.

NED   Maybe.

PHIL   Maybe?

NED   I think you should know. Just to reassure you. Your Josh won't let you down.

PHIL   And how the fuck would you know?

NED   Because he showed me what he's capable of. Earlier. Just to pass the time. And I was amazed. He's won the big challenge.

PHIL   Oh and what's that?

NED   Found his own voice.

PHIL   That pip-squeak? Well, I'm more than thrilled for him.

NED   Really generous of you.

PHIL   And I wish him the best.

NED   You're not going to stay and sample it?

PHIL   If he hadn't the decency to include me in on this. To share this skill, this very special and personal talent. With his own father, then why should I? He can go out there and die the death.

NED   Maybe you're right, Phil.

PHIL   I know I'm right.

NED   And I was telling lies. Josh did show me his act. Worse set I've ever seen in my life.

PHIL   No?

NED   Appalling.

PHIL   Worse than Eamon?

NED   'Fraid so.

PHIL   Then let him go out there and die the death twice over. And good riddance. Time I put all this behind me. This is goodbye.

NED   Where will you go?

PHIL   Prague.

NED   Don't be silly.

PHIL   Best decision I'll ever make.

NED   This is your home.

PHIL   What man in England recognises his home anymore? Eh? I'm one of many. You can see it in the eyes. Fear. Regret. Blame. We're finished. Broken. We've lost the ability to be brave and stand up for what we believe in. So Eastern Europe here I come.

NED   "Phil of Prague"? Not exactly bums on seats.

PHIL   I'm going down the fire escape. When I came up, even the back door had kitchen staff lingering. Don't want to face any of them. Not anymore.

NED   Bugger off then.

PHIL   Where is it? Any idea? Did you make your health and safety checks?

NED   Through the Gents. Next door.

PHIL   Bye, Ned. You've been a godsend to me.

NED   Ring your GP. You asked me to remind
   you.

PHIL   I have done.

NED   And what did he have to say?

PHIL   Mind your own business.

*PHIL leaves with his bags and Percy. NED gazes into his
tablet and clicks. The light flashes up again to his face.*

NED   Who's he trying to kid? You are not bubbly
   and fun. You've got the eyes of a sex maniac. Who can't
   deliver the goods.

PHIL returns. NED still looks at his screen.

PHIL   Second thoughts, Ned.

NED   Yes?

PHIL   Is he really bad?

NED   Yes.

PHIL   Like really, really bad?

NED   Embarrassing.

PHIL   How come?

NED   He hasn't learnt from his father's example.
   Doesn't bag the jewels of your experience. There were
   times I had to cover my eyes. Or turn away. Terrible.

PHIL   And he's ready to go out there?

NED   Oh yes.

PHIL   It will destroy him.

NED   He wouldn't listen.

PHIL   Completely. Believe me, I know. This is not an easy job. Not only do you have to be very funny, live comedy needs a unique stage presence, a talent to reveal the ordinary in a very special way. And although it sounds so American, and let's face it, that's where stand up originated, you have to invest in and expose your own pain.

NED   Which is your speciality. And I'm afraid poor Josh doesn't go deep enough.

PHIL   Too indulged. Privileged. Getting it wrong. But getting away with it.

NED   If I'm honest, if he goes out there tonight, he'll be annihilated. *(His tablet 'pings'.)* 'Dalston Paul'? A response.

PHIL puts his bags down. He kisses Percy.

PHIL   No father could let that happen to his son.

NED   No way.

PHIL   Poor chap. To be so self-deluded.

NED   Very common in your profession.

PHIL   To take that risk in front of Ria.

NED   His precious girl.

PHIL   His mother.

NED   Your manager. Spotted in the bar. Keen to have you back?

PHIL   Think so? Apart from anything else, I have to consider my reputation. With every good will in the world I couldn't let my own son humiliate himself. Or indeed ruin this opportunity.

NED   I couldn't agree more.

PHIL   Oh Christ. *(He just stands frozen to the spot.)* What lies on the bottom of the ocean and twitches? A nervous wreck. Look at the state of me. Numb. Disbelieving. Panic stricken. Everything has gone blank. No idea where to begin.

NED still on his tablet.

NED   What about..?

PHIL   Save me.

NED   Pets that fill a void?

PHIL   Eh?

NED   People using pets, say like a parrot, to fill a void?

PHIL   Huh? Not me. Besides these new hot producers are looking for someone who takes chances. I saw a comic online at the BBC Radio New Comedy show this year. Apparently he couldn't remember a thing of what he rehearsed. So he improvised like crazy for five minutes about some hot date with a girl whose field was breath. "My work is breath," she said. It was total nonsense but he riffed it beautifully.

PHIL   Packed with clever word-play and surrealism. He even got the audience checking their own for halitosis. And I thought "Blimey, you have to have balls of steel to throw away a polished set you've been honing, for however long."

NED closes his tablet.

NED   Take my word for it, Phil. You're quite capable. Give it a go. Best of British. *(Beat)* But then I know you. That also won't be quite good enough, will it?

PHIL   Some other person's shit? Nah.

NED   You will find your own material. Even at a moment's notice.

PHIL   Indeed I will.

NED *(looking at his watch)* In less than five minutes.

PHIL lets out a terrible groan.

NED   It wasn't what you wanted to hear? From the 'Doc'? Was it?

PHIL   Don't go there. *(Beat)* But then why not? A taboo subject? A potent uncertainty? An ever -increasing threat to the UK's male population? Just leave it with me, Neddie.

NED quietly leaves. PHIL alone. He focuses. He kisses Percy. He genuflects before the mirror.

He takes one last swig of any remaining beer. He pulls out a bottle of water and turns out the lights.

He opens the door and stands in the bright light from the landing. An announcement:

"Ladies and Gentlemen, give it up for..."

Blackout.

SCENE 3

It continues dark. We hear some of PHIL's act:

PHIL   "It was two in the morning. I'd had a couple of scotches the evening before. It usually works. I woke up hard as a rock. I put my hand on Pete, my cock, but within seconds it went away. The erection. That light bulb flashing even for a man of my age, can still be a joy. But no. Pete settled back.

And said, "We need to talk, Phil." I was immediately concerned.

Guys, look guys we all know aimless chatting can put us off our stroke.

Unless it's smut. Pete continued, gently almost, 'We need to talk. Listen, let me first say, it's not you. It's me. It really is. You're a smashing chap. You've been a great friend to me. Generous lover. Marvellous company. But after much careful thought, I think we should call it a day. We've had some wonderful times. Taken me in hand. Rubbed me up the right way. But...all good things must come to an end. We need to move on. You need to move on.'

Does this all seem familiar? Eh? Heart to heart with the beloved? Then a few weeks later. Same thing. Two o'clock in the morning. Woke up. I might add... Pete and I were back together again.

I don't give up that easily. Anyway, Pete moaned about not seeing his friends anymore. So I tackled that. More pornography.

More online sex chat. The odd prostitute. Real and virtual.

Even back with an ex for a month or so. But clearly something still wasn't quite right. Pete gave me a look. And this time it was sinister.

He wasn't going to rise up to the occasion. He just lay there. Feeling sorry for himself. I thought this is serious. Damn serious.

My pal Pete, used to have a mind of his own and now he was almost begging for help. Professional help. Therapy even?

I don't know. So after much deliberation, I called my GP. He told me the person in the waiting room that really needs to be seen first, is not the sick child, not the pregnant woman, it's absolutely the adult male. Why? It's taken a lot of courage and pain, to drag himself there. Most men are shit-scared when they have to finally admit there's something physically wrong with them.

And down there, well us blokes have to learn to accept, the older we get, it becomes more and more of a war zone – the land of the knob. Agreed? And maybe when it's sorted, all that remains...'

An odd thump, huge laughter, then abrupt silence, as if something has broken. Vivid street light, bleeding in through the curtains. We find LIZ, drinking Campari, and checking her iphone. She pockets it and turns on the lights. She then moves to the make-shift dressing table and scans it.

RIA has forgotten her e-cigarette. She doesn't check herself in the mirror.

She sees PHIL's gown in a heap on the floor. She hesitates then puts her Campari down on the table. She picks up the gown and places it over the chair.

RIA enters suddenly glimpsing this.

RIA   Sorry.

LIZ picks up RIA's e-cigarette.

LIZ   This what you're looking for?

RIA   Thanks.

LIZ *(hands it to Ria)* Phil's not tried that one before. Falling off the stage.

RIA   Will he be alright, do you think?

LIZ   As usual the crowd didn't bat an eyelid. Thought it was part of the act. Without question, biggest laugh this evening.

NED rushes in and collects PHIL's gown over the chair.

NED   He'll live.

LIZ   Who was that giving my ex the kiss of life?

NED   The landlord, Modo.

LIZ   That can't be his real name surely?

RIA   Who cares? He got him back.

LIZ   He was pretending.

NED *(To RIA)* No need to worry, pet.

LIZ   It was light concussion. He just wanted sympathy.

NED   The Modo is an ex-nurse, apparently. He's full of surprises. Guess what? He was thrilled with the show. And can you believe it, if Phil's fit, he wants him back tomorrow? It being Saturday, there should be more regulars in.

NED leaves forgetting the door.

LIZ   I do wish that man would get over my husband.

RIA   His heart's in the right place.

LIZ   But it's been going on for years. He even had a bandage in his bag. And what kind of man carries lint? I saw him sniffing it once. That robe.

RIA   Perhaps it needed a wash.

LIZ   If they can't get their hands on anything else, fans like Ned, having muscled their way in, make themselves indispensable. *(Beat)*

RIA   Can I buy you a drink?

LIZ   I've still got my Campari, thanks.

LIZ collects her glass from the table. RIA heads for the door.

LIZ   Don't run away.

RIA   I'm not. Come with me.

LIZ   Actually, I...

RIA   Join me downstairs.

LIZ   I'm hiding from all the palaver below, you see. Keep me company. *(She closes the door.)* Until things quieten down? Please?

RIA   Sure. I'll let in some air though. Stuffy.

RIA opens the curtains and the window. She vapes.

LIZ   Thank you so much.

RIA   What for?

LIZ   Making this evening happen. It was a complete success.

RIA   I do my very best.

LIZ   And you've got some delightful friends.

RIA   They're an excellent crowd. *(She sits.)*

LIZ   What do you make of Josh's particular talent?

RIA   His attempts at stand up? He's good. From what I've seen. Do you think he might have a future?

LIZ   A question I was going to ask you.

RIA   He's got a lot to learn. But why not? He should have a crack at it. Don't you think?

LIZ   If the opportunity arises.

RIA   Baby steps first. No rush.

LIZ   Absolutely. It did cross my mind though, with your lovely contacts, you might now fight his corner?

RIA   Julia's here to focus on Phil, I suspect. When he's on form, nobody can touch him. In my humble opinion. Ever since I was a girl and first saw him, every Saturday night on television, I was obsessed. With his act, what he said made sense to me. I got it.

LIZ   He's very lucky to have your support.

RIA   I think we're all here to help each other. Don't you?

LIZ   It's a jungle out there. *(Beat)* What is that?

RIA   Steam.

LIZ   And the smell?

RIA   'Tropical Fruits.' My favourite.

LIZ   Delicious.

RIA   It can be a very successful smoke-screen.

LIZ   I imagine so. *(Beat)* Can I just say how thrilled I am that you and Josh have sorted things.

RIA   It would take a lot to pull us apart.

LIZ   It's been on my mind. I just couldn't quite understand why you fell out.

RIA   In the end, neither could I. He means a lot to me. As I know he does to you. No disrespect, but I would say he's still tied to his mother's apron strings a little.

LIZ   I've never worn a pinafore in my life.

RIA   And it did him the world of good to see his father in action again.

LIZ   Think so?

RIA   Did you and Phil manage to have a chat?

LIZ   When?

RIA   Before the show?

LIZ   That would make him too nervous. We're not exactly chums anymore. To put it mildly.

RIA   But you still love him? Yeh?

LIZ   What makes you say that?

RIA   We can never let them go. Can we? The men in our lives. If we're forced to.

LIZ   I sense that Josh would prefer old wounds to be healed so I made every effort to be here.

RIA   Appreciate that. Totally.

LIZ   I could never trust him, you see. Not in the end. He was such a liar. You can't sustain a marriage on lies.

RIA   No way.

LIZ   Barefaced lies about fidelity and such. Love goes out of the window.

RIA stands and if possible, moves back to the window.

RIA   You can forgive.

LIZ   Can you?

RIA   I'm capable of forgiving.

LIZ   Who have you to forgive?

RIA   My mother.

LIZ   Right.

RIA   She walked out on us and took everything. But not Ria. There was me. Dad. And my hedgehog Reggie. And Phil's TV show, which I watched with Dad's finger up my arse. And that was my life for most of my teen years.

LIZ   But you seem so well-adjusted.

RIA   I had a spot of therapy. I had a desperate need to be loved, I was told. Who hasn't? Then I thought why am I paying a complete stranger when you can talk to a friend over coffee? For free. Maybe we should do that some time?

LIZ   I'd love to. *(Beat)* I do admire you. You seem so confident.

RIA   Believe me, it's an act.

LIZ   You have a good job. You dress well. You are back with your boyfriend. And my God, you have a very special relationship with his father. An extremely complicated and difficult personality. What next, I ask myself?

RIA   A double act?

LIZ   A magician's assistant?

RIA   He cuts me in half.

LIZ   Throws knives at you.

RIA   While I'm pinned to a moving target. I'd let him do almost anything. I respect him.

LIZ   He's lost none of his charm.

RIA   Like father, like son. And it's no surprise that they both make us laugh. That's special. Important. And a good giggle keeps the demons at bay. Don't you think?

LIZ   Yes.

RIA   Smashing chat, Liz. Let's pick it up another time? *(She goes to the door.)*

LIZ   Sure. But don't go. Confidentially, I need to ask you something.

RIA   I really should be with my mates. See if Josh is doing OK?

LIZ   Did my husband jump on you?

RIA   Sorry?

LIZ   Did you sleep with Phil?

RIA   Please don't insult me, Liz. What do you take me for? I know he has a reputation. I don't. I'd never dream of it.

LIZ   Yes, it would get rather messy. But I'm trying to understand why you've done so much for him and less for Josh. Why are you bothering with him?

RIA   I'm lost, darling. Who?

LIZ   Well, you tell me. Mmm? He looked so unhappy down there.

RIA   Josh?

LIZ   I could tell there was a lot on his mind. He was perfectly fine when we met earlier. Now I have to say he looks terribly upset.

RIA   Then let me sort him out?

LIZ   Have you any idea what could have happened? He even appeared annoyed with Phil in some way. For instance, he wasn't really laughing tonight. Didn't you notice?

RIA   No.

LIZ   Perhaps you were more concerned about, I don't know, Julia's reaction?

RIA   Might have been.

LIZ   Or worried that you had gone too far? Far too far.

RIA   What you on about, woman? *(Beat)*

LIZ   What amuses one can be very revealing. Speaks volumes.

RIA   I'm in no mood for a lecture.

LIZ   Every moment of Phil's act tonight filled you with excitement. The more vulgar he became, the more you wet yourself. It was like some extraordinary exorcism.

RIA   And it never once had that effect on you?

LIZ   I confess. That's why I recognised it. A ridiculous infatuation. So let's not allow history to repeat itself?

Now LIZ opens the door but remains in front of it.

RIA ends her vaping.

LIZ   Is this why you split from Josh? Only then to decide to have him back? I mean why would a sensible hard-working girl like you...? Who already had a 'decent' relationship with a young man, gainfully employed, handsome, not living with his parents, allow somebody like his father into your bed?

RIA   You're talking riddles, Liz.

LIZ   Does Josh know? I think he suspects. And it might break him in two. Not for the first time. I beat you to it. I told him his father was a scum-bag. No mother should treat her child like that.

RIA   That's enough.

LIZ   How dare you?

RIA   Stop it.

LIZ   How dare you show your face this evening. And act as if you're doing nothing but good.

RIA   How can I convince you, I want only the best for him?

LIZ   Again? Who? Which one?

RIA   My lad.

LIZ   Break with him.

RIA   I love him.

LIZ   And face the consequences.

Silence except for the noise from the street.

RIA   Did he really look sad down there?

LIZ   It was the reason I had to share it with you. I couldn't bear it. *(Beat)* Do what you can. Make sure your super-duper friend is aware of Josh's gifts.

RIA   I've told you. Julia's attention is elsewhere.

LIZ   Then divert it. He needs a change. Maybe it's not the only reason, but he doesn't enjoy his job anymore. He wants to follow in his father's footsteps.

Professionally we hope. Comedy is in his genes and none of us have any right to supress it. But there's a difference. Phil sadly equates being a successful stand-up with sexual conquest. His big mistake in the past and why he gained a stinking reputation. Is talent scout Julia aware of that?

RIA   How should I know?

LIZ   She wouldn't be very pleased to hear it.

RIA   Why don't you mind your own fucking business? You're just pissed off your marriage collapsed.

LIZ   Oh come on, I got over that one years ago. *(Beat)* Now I can't do much for the planet, but I can still save my son. And so can you. Before jumping ship? It's the least you can do, for your gross misdemeanours in the past... Your greed perhaps at wanting everything on offer. And almost getting away with it? Don't you think?

PHIL is led in by NED through the open door.

He suffers cuts and bruises expertly dressed.

PHIL   Do you mind? I've got a business meeting.

LIZ   Haven't had one of those for a while.

PHIL   What are you doing here?

LIZ   You and I must have a chat.

PHIL   No way. People need to see me. Now.

PHIL sits down.

NED   Modo wants to bend your ear.

PHIL   He wants to what?

NED   He wants to have you tomorrow evening.

LIZ   We are popular.

PHIL   Shut up.

LIZ   We have to talk about Josh.

PHIL   What does he actually want?

NED   Just a friendly chat.

PHIL   Stay close to me, Ned.

NED   I'm here for you.

LIZ   Oh give us a break.

PHIL   To actually come round and find the Modo with his tongue down my throat, I'm amazed I live to tell the tale.

NED   You bumped your head badly.

PHIL   Why was he giving me the kiss of life?

NED   He fancies you.

PHIL   If I'm honest I didn't need it.

NED   Maybe he was just covering every option.

PHIL   I was taken advantage of.

LIZ   Makes a refreshing change.

PHIL   I was vulnerable and exposed. I blame my manager. I'm going to the press. Appear on a chat show. Enhance my reputation.

LIZ   A private word everybody, with the injured party.

PHIL   Please don't leave me with her. She's been drinking.

LIZ looks at her iphone to check the time.

LIZ   It must be last orders. Ned, be an angel and get me another Campari.

LIZ hands NED cash. PHIL clocks this.

RIA   Is Josh downstairs?

NED   The last I saw of him he was in deep conversation with that Julia.

LIZ *(to RIA)* You have a head start, my girl.

RIA leaves. NED follows closing the door.

LIZ   You are the most self-deluded idiot I have ever known.

PHIL   I was a triumph out there.

LIZ   You look like an extra from Hitchcock's 'The Birds'.

PHIL   I'm shattered.

LIZ   I'm sending Josh up now so you can apologise.

PHIL   What for?

LIZ   You ruined our marriage, why destroy the potential for his?

PHIL   Still blaming me?

LIZ   Of course I am.

PHIL   You treated me like a second-class citizen.

LIZ   That's because you behave like one.

PHIL   There are those that think England a class-ridden society. And those who think it doesn't matter either way. As long as you know your place in the game. You remain one of the latter.

LIZ   Only because I've worked harder than most to be independent. An agenda you approved of when we married, so you could sit back, make the most of it and exploit me.

PHIL   While still having the time to smother my son.

LIZ   Why? Because you were hardly around.

PHIL   I saw the mistakes Josh was making.

LIZ   Well, he didn't really have a good start with us as parents.

PHIL   Not least of all his choice in women.

LIZ   I agree, but you still stole his property.

PHIL   How do you know?

LIZ   I've learnt to keep my ears and eyes open.

PHIL   It was my last-ditch attempt to save him.

LIZ   How fascinating. From what?

PHIL   She's a banker.

LIZ   Some credit to her.

PHIL   And he's an estate agent.

LIZ   Lucrative professions.

PHIL   Deadly combination.

LIZ   You've still destroyed any romance as far as he's concerned.

PHIL   Then in my opinion, an evening of unqualified success.

LIZ *(suddenly)* How could you do this to him?

PHIL   Can we move on?

LIZ   How low could you sink?

PHIL   Keep your bloody voice down.

LIZ   You should be castrated.

PHIL   Might not be any further need for that, love.

LIZ   Arsehole. *(Beat)* Please. Say sorry. At least.

PHIL   And that will make him feel better?

LIZ   Never. But it's a start.

PHIL   And what do I get in return?

LIZ   What a question coming from a father.

PHIL   There has to be something in it for me.

LIZ   This is not some crappy deal.

PHIL   Knowing you, I'm unconvinced.

LIZ   Josh worships the ground you tread on. I suppose in a way, that's what it should be. If you don't apologise tonight, get down on bended knee, it will finish him. And I'll do whatever it takes to finish you.

PHIL   How?

LIZ   Introduce myself to Julia Trevis and disclose a few home truths.

Pause.

PHIL   How is life, Liz?

LIZ   Wonderful without you. Still.

PHIL   Then why come back for more?

LIZ   Initially, to please my son. See if he's coping.

PHIL   That's it, you see. In a nutshell. You put him before me. Always. As you are doing now.

LIZ I had no alternative. You were such a poor investment.

PHIL That lad became the world to you. You pushed me out. Refused to have sex. For four years we were sleeping in separate rooms. I never ever stopped wanting you. Despite your politics and your selfishness and your ambition. I hear you now run the family business. Single-handed. Your brother, always kind to me, has left the country. Your mother is in a home. Admittedly the best, but Josh tells me when he visits all she ever talks about and wants to see, is you. 'Where is she? Where is your mother?' She asks over and over again. Like a tiny lost girl. In tears. I recall the same feeling.

A knock on the door.

PHIL (*calling*) Ned?

LIZ Go away.

PHIL (*to LIZ*) This is my dressing room. Do you mind?

LIZ Will you beg Josh for forgiveness?

PHIL I'll try. (*He stands.*) He'll still smash my face in. I would.

LIZ Then I suggest you offer him something.

PHIL I've got nothing.

LIZ Actually, not strictly true. For once.

PHIL What then?

LIZ You could share the gig tomorrow evening.

PHIL Get lost.

LIZ Give him a chance. He's good.

PHIL   Ned says he's awful.

LIZ   That was to get you on tonight.

PHIL   How do you know?

LIZ   He told me.

PHIL   The traitor. I'll think about it. And by the way, you look sensational.

LIZ   Thank you.

PHIL   Can I ask a favour?

LIZ   By all means.

PHIL   I need a bed for the night.

LIZ   Out of the question.

LIZ opens the door. NED was behind it. He holds LIZ's Campari.

PHIL   Yes?

NED *(to PHIL)* Julia wants you. She only has five minutes.

LIZ   Not sure he can manage that anymore. *(She grabs the Campari.)* Goodnight.

She leaves.

NED enters.

PHIL   I need a quiet moment, Ned.

NED   Boss.

NED sharply leaves, closing the door.

PHIL checks his iphone for texts then puts it down. He waits a second then grabs Percy. He gently turns him over, unties the back, and pulls out cash. He pockets it.

He leaves forgetting his iphone on the dressing table.

The door remains open.

SCENE 4

Ten minutes later. We might see a fading Union Jack on a pole through the open window. A 'Last Orders' bell can be heard ringing then ends. JOSH and RIA face each other in the room, the door now closed. RIA is not vaping.

JOSH   Was that it? Trying to justify why we were a couple in the first place?

RIA   If you like.

JOSH   Was that your reason for breaking up? Yes?

RIA   Could have been.

JOSH   What then?

RIA   Look, we're now back together. Right?

JOSH   For certain?

RIA   What we want. Both of us. And apologies again for putting you through it. (*Pause.*)

JOSH   Thanks for persuading Julia to see Dad tonight. Do him a lot of good.

RIA   Mission accomplished.

JOSH   I really like her.

RIA   She knows what she's doing.

JOSH   We had a nice chat downstairs. She said you put in a good word for me.

RIA   Yes.

JOSH   Why?

RIA   Because you're talented, darling.

JOSH   I showed her some of my material on my phone. Bits and pieces. Just making the lads giggle at work. She was very encouraging. Cheered me up no end. Thanks again for all your hard work. Appreciate that. *(Beat)* Before she left the pub, Mom said dad wanted to see me. What about?

RIA   How should I know? By the way, he's not well, your old man.

JOSH   What's wrong?

RIA   Ask him. Ned says he's been having tests. Scans. They've found something.

JOSH   Not contagious is it?

RIA   Hardly think so. Waterworks.

JOSH   Turned out to be a bit of an arse evening.

RIA   Well, we've survived?

JOSH   If you say so.

PHIL enters. RIA makes a move to leave.

JOSH *(to RIA)* Where you going?

PHIL   Josh?

JOSH   I've not finished.

RIA *(to JOSH)* Now what?

Then PHIL looks at RIA. JOSH clocks this immediately.

JOSH   Hello? Another look. Bit different that one, team. No longer the look of lust?

RIA *(to JOSH)* Totally inaccurate.

JOSH   What?

RIA   Give people the benefit of the doubt.

JOSH *(to RIA)* You haven't a leg to stand on.

RIA   Turn the fucking page, will you?

PHIL   Stop this.

RIA   Tossers. The pair of you. You deserve each other. *(She heads for the door.)* I'm off.

PHIL   Now pack it in. Like a couple of kids. Kiss and make up. Believe me, life's too short. *(He grabs his iphone from the dressing table.)* Can I get anybody a drink? Before they lock up for the night?

JOSH and RIA freeze. PHIL is going to put his hand in his pocket. A rare moment. They both shake their heads declining.

PHIL   Please yourselves. And when I get back, I'd like a quick word, lad.

PHIL leaves. Silence except for the street. JOSH and RIA now look at each other. Then JOSH finds his engagement ring.

JOSH   Sorry. Sorry. My argument should never have been with you. *(He shows it to her.)* Please marry me? Please be my wife.

RIA   Look love.

JOSH   I'm proposing.

RIA   Got that.

JOSH   I believe you. I believe what you said. All of it. We can't build a marriage on lies. One of us will eventually walk out. *(Pause. He reaches for her hand.)*

RIA   You're shaking.

JOSH   You still have no idea what this means to me.

RIA   I do. Now.

JOSH is about to put on the ring. RIA hesitates then her hand falls.

RIA   No.

JOSH   No?

RIA   It's too soon.

JOSH   I don't think so.

RIA   Give it awhile.

JOSH   Marry me.

RIA   Listen, I've a lot to sort out. Been a massive evening for all of us.

JOSH   If you refuse me, I know in my heart that my father, my own father, took you away from me.

RIA   He didn't. He couldn't. I'm here. Now let it go. Please.

JOSH   That moment. Before the show. You were not. Mine.

RIA   Why would I even let him?

JOSH   God knows.

RIA   Why would I lie to you?

JOSH   I left the room. You asked me to leave the room. To be alone with a man who yes, you might know a thing or two about, and admire, but...

RIA   Yes?

JOSH   I didn't see a woman who didn't want to be there. And his expression was of complete joy. He couldn't wait. For the first time this evening Dad was his old smug self. Mixing business with pleasure. So unprofessional.

RIA   Why would he be interested? In the first place?

JOSH   You are gorgeous. You are a match for him. And you are everything to me.

RIA   Then surely he wouldn't dream of it?

JOSH   He would want you because I want you. And because he's not half the man he used to be. Not able to pull anymore. Mid-life crisis and all that. And to have his own back for me loving my mom. Still. Like I love you. Like I've always loved you. *(Beat)* Ria? Just say you'll marry me?

RIA   You deserve better. You do. No. (Her iphone 'pings'. She looks at it.) Julia. I need to speak to her.

JOSH   What for?

RIA   She needs me.

JOSH   What for?

RIA   I don't know. *(Beat)* She's a manipulative cow your old lady.

JOSH   Well, I made every effort to break away. And failed.

RIA and JOSH remain still and silent.

We hear the noise from the street. Then RIA leaves. JOSH remains, undecided what to do. He then suddenly throws the ring out of the window.

PHIL returns with a large pint.

PHIL   Fancy one? Are you sure? They're still serving.

JOSH   I'm off the booze. Don't you ever listen to me?

PHIL   Beg pardon. That's right.

JOSH   Have you been paid?

PHIL   Not that kind of gig, was it?

PHIL drinks.

JOSH   How did your meeting go?

PHIL   What meeting?

JOSH   With Trevis?

PHIL   Texting me. Yeh. Maybe cooling down a bit already. (*He sips his pint.*) Josh?

JOSH   Hello?

PHIL   I slept with Ria.

JOSH   I know. How was it?

PHIL   Since you asked, couldn't get it up. Not surprising really. Even for a cunt like me. Did she mention that?

JOSH   No.

PHIL   That's decent of her. I am so sorry.

JOSH   So am I.

PHIL   It was nothing, Josh. For me, a final flourish. Even then, a big fat flop at the first hurdle. I'm sure any damage can be repaired.

JOSH   We'll see. (*Beat*) I'm a tosser now. We both are. Cheers, Dad.

PHIL   I will do everything...

JOSH   You've done enough, mate.

PHIL   Will you forgive me?

JOSH   Big ask, Pop.

PHIL puts his pint down.

PHIL   Then why don't you hit me?

JOSH   Why?

PHIL   Come on. I deserve it.

JOSH   Take a look in the mirror. Be like kicking a dead man.

PHIL   Nice one.

PHIL puts his arms around JOSH. JOSH takes the hug but doesn't really respond. PHIL holding him still, pats him on the back. JOSH breaks it. He looks at his iphone.

PHIL   I'm at a loose end tonight. We could have a bite to eat. On me. Talk things through.

JOSH   Like?

PHIL   My health issues.

JOSH   You fell over. On stage. Get over it.

PHIL   On top of that.

JOSH   Must be payback time then.

PHIL   One way of looking at it. Have to have an operation.

JOSH   When?

PHIL   Lap of the Gods at the moment with the NHS.

JOSH   Keep me posted.

PHIL   Actually, I need a place to put my head down for the night. I'm homeless.

JOSH has found a short video on his iphone. He hands it to PHIL.

JOSH   Take a look. Go on. Take a look.

PHIL takes the iphone. We can just hear a sound track. Men are laughing. We hear JOSH's voice.

PHIL   What's this?

JOSH   Me messing about at work.

PHIL *(smiles)* Didn't know you went in for this kind of thing?

JOSH   Thought I might have a go.

PHIL   Interesting.

JOSH   Hooked already on 'joke coke', Pop.

PHIL *(hands the iphone back to JOSH)* Tomorrow night?

JOSH   Yeh?

PHIL   How do you feel about maybe...

JOSH finds another short video.

JOSH   What time's your meeting? With money bags, Julia?

PHIL   I told you. She said she'd text me.

JOSH   Take another look.

PHIL   Daddy's very tired, son.

JOSH   One last look.

PHIL takes the iphone and watches the video. More of JOSH's mates laughing. PHIL doesn't respond.

JOSH   She's seeing me at lunchtime. Monday lunchtime. Because of my job and that.

PHIL   Who is?

JOSH   Julia. I showed her this on my phone. She loved it. Do you love it, Dad?

PHIL   Not the point, is it? Not bad. Not really my cup of tea.

JOSH   She seemed to like it. The look of it. Think she took a shine to me.

PHIL   She's certainly very keen on Ria.

JOSH   Who can blame her? Reckon us chaps have lost the plot.

PHIL   Sort of know where you're coming from.

JOSH   That's a first.

PHIL   Actually, this is why I gave it a go. Testing her. Safeguarding you. Thinking she might be unfaithful.

JOSH lurches to PHIL, as if he's going to hit him. PHIL flinches. Then JOSH simply takes the iphone from him.

JOSH   My meeting must be after yours.

PHIL   What is she proposing?

JOSH   Proposing?

PHIL   What exactly does she have in mind for you?

JOSH   Have to wait and see.

PHIL   Well done, lad.

JOSH   Thanks Dad. You proud of me?

PHIL   Always room at the top.

JOSH   She mentioned your mate, Eamon. Turned up tonight I think.

PHIL   That bastard was out there?

JOSH   Came and went apparently. (*PHIL finds his pint and drinks.*) She might set up a meeting with him. Said something about me writing him fresh material. She didn't know you were best buddies. You don't mind, do you? I don't want to tread on anybody's toes.

PHIL   As I said, son. The offer is there.

JOSH   What offer?

PHIL   We go out there together.

JOSH   Out where?

PHIL   Combine forces. Tomorrow night. That's what the gig is for apparently.

JOSH   A double act? Share and share alike, eh?

PHIL   Give it a whirl? A try out? Why not? Nothing to lose.

JOSH   Ah... Too soon, Dad.

PHIL   Please yourself. (*Beat*) You really got your heart set on this game then? If you don't get signed up, it's really tough.

JOSH   The comedy industry is now worth millions a year. Thanks to sell-out stadium tours, game shows, DVD sales, book deals. I want a slice of the pie. Like everybody else. And shed-loads in the bank before I'm thirty.

PHIL   Not everyone is earning big money.

JOSH   So that's why I need more time. Grow wings. Fly off the perch.

PHIL   I warn you, most drop out, three years after starting. But I can wait.

JOSH   Hoped you might. Then I really will fucking kick you in the balls.

JOSH leaves closing the door. PHIL alone, still, almost frozen. A tap on the door. PHIL doesn't respond. He stares into the mirror.

NED enters quietly. He puts his tablet in his bag and maybe other bits and pieces.

PHIL   How's my Neddie?

NED   Not bad.

PHIL *(drinks)* Fancy one?

NED   Eh?

PHIL   Drink on me?

NED   Er... Another time, Phil. I'll be off now.

PHIL   Where to?

NED   Nothing much left to do, is there?

PHIL   Was I good?

NED   They loved you.

PHIL   And where did they all come from?

NED   We had a ring around.

PHIL   Magic. I was flying again. Cheers, pal. *(Beat)* Where are you off to then? Some club?

NED   Don't do that anymore. I walk in, buy a drink, and just stand there. It's as if I don't exist. The ghost nobody wants to see. Hardly get a look and never catch anybody's eye. But where there's a will there's a way. Thanks to the internet.

PHIL   Did think about joining you.

NED   What for?

PHIL   Dunno. Few laughs. See how the night goes. Feeling a bit... down?

NED   After tonight? Come on. *(puts a hand on his shoulder)* Now save your energy for tomorrow.

PHIL   What if I come back to yours?

NED   Mmm?

PHIL   I need to crash down somewhere.

NED   Bit short notice.

PHIL   Sorry to off-load like this. But you had a sofa bed you said. For when your sister stays?

NED   Collapsed. Not Barbara, the bed. Been meaning to replace it. Only a cheapie from Ikea.

PHIL   Getting biblical, this search for a room. Tell you what? I'll get in with you.

NED   In where?

PHIL   Your bed. We're grown men, Ned. I know what I'm doing. Maybe it's time to... Give it a go? Before it's too late. Bob Hoskins did it in a sauna once.

NED   Did he?

PHIL   Play it by ear. Chill out. See what happens. I hasten to add, there won't be much action from me. And it will be very safe. You might have to do all the donkey work. As you've hinted before, you can be a very patient man. With your taste for seniors. *(Beat)* Don't tell me you're not up to it?

NED   I've got a date.

PHIL   You?

NED   I know.

PHIL   Thought you said. Fuck me. How come?

NED   Site I never normally bother with. Meeting him in ten minutes. 'Dalston Paul'.

PHIL   Maybe I could watch. Join in? Is he... like young? Like a girl?

NED   Hairy, in his early fifties and a bouncer.

PHIL   No, ta.

NED   Tell you what, though. I could have a word with Modo on the way down. He's locking up.

PHIL   This goes from bad to worse.

NED   What I mean is, you could spend the night here.

PHIL   With him? In this piss pen?

NED   I could explain the situation. On your behalf if you like. He can be very accommodating. *(He scans the room.)* Bit dusty, but it's OK. A loo on the same floor. It's even got a sofa. He'll find you a blanket.

PHIL   Oh the kindness of strangers.

NED   He thinks you're amazing. Don't say I said anything.

PHIL   No fear.

NED *(moves to the window and looks out)* Clear night.

PHIL   Is it?

NED   What's she doing?

PHIL   Who?

NED   Ria. Rushing off? Along the pavement? On her own? *(He closes the window.)* Another thing...

PHIL   Break it to me gently.

NED   Sadly, I won't be free. Not tomorrow.

PHIL   Won't need you until about eight, buddy.

NED   I'd like to keep my options open.

PHIL   You've got options?

NED   I'm feeling very hopeful about tonight. His profile suggests he likes to take things... slowly. He's looking for commitment. A relationship. Marriage? And well... It is the weekend, after all. It might take time. So I hope it all...

PHIL   Yeh?

NED   The gig. Always great to be asked back.

PHIL   True.

NED   Modo says you'll put his 'Albion Pub' back on the map. You took the place by storm. Turned the evening round. Against all odds. You'll be doing corporative jobs soon and you won't want to know me.

PHIL   Give you a bell then?

NED   When?

PHIL   In the week?

NED   If you like.

PHIL   Have a good one.

NED   Bye, Phil.

NED leaves.

PHIL stares into the mirror. He reaches for his pint, then doesn't drink it. Then a knock on the door.

PHIL   Hello? Yes? What do you want?

Blackout.

The end.

Aurora Metro Books

HAMLET adapted by Mark Norfolk
ISBN 978-1-911501-01-5 £9.99

COMBUSTION by Asif Khan
ISBN 978-1-911501-91-6 £9.99

DIARY OF A HOUNSLOW GIRL by Ambreen Razia
ISBN 978-0-9536757-9-1 £8.99

SPLIT/MIXED by Ery Nzaramba
ISBN 978-1-911501-97-8 £10.99

A GIRL WITH A BOOK by Nick Wood
ISBN 978-1-910798-61-4 £12.99

THE TROUBLE WITH ASIAN MEN by Sudha Bhuchar, Kristine Landon-Smith and Louise Wallinger
ISBN 978-1-906582-41-8 £8.99

SOUTHEAST ASIAN PLAYS ed. Cheryl Robson and Aubrey Mellor
ISBN 978-1-906582-86-9 £16.99

SIX PLAYS BY BLACK AND ASIAN WOMEN WRITERS ed. Kadija George
ISBN 978-0-9515877-2-0 £12.99

DURBAN DIALOGUES, INDIAN VOICE by Ashwin Singh
ISBN 978-1-906582-42-5 £15.99

WOMEN OF ASIA by Asa Palomera
ISBN 978-1-906582-94-4 £7.99

HARVEST by Manjula Padmanabhan
ISBN 978-0-9536757-7-7 £6.99

I HAVE BEFORE ME A REMARKABLE DOCUMENT by Sonja Linden
ISBN 978-0-9546912-3-3 £7.99

THE IRANIAN FEAST by Kevin Dyer
ISBN 978-1-910798-93-5 £8.99

NEW SOUTH AFRICAN PLAYS ed. Charles J. Fourie
ISBN 978-0-9542330-1-3 £11.99

BLACK AND ASIAN PLAYS Anthology introduced by Afia Nkrumah
ISBN 978-0-9536757-4-6 £12.99

www.aurorametro.com